D1571773

PRAISE FOR
RELATIONSHIPS AT WORK

"Rachel B. Simon walks the walk in this unique spin on networking that doesn't ask us to compromise our identities. The email templates and tips scattered throughout the book provide examples demonstrating that she can show as much as tell, and can lead us to a new way of thinking about how we can network and be ourselves at the same time."

—**David Satchell**, author of *Extracting the Leader from Within*

"At a time when more of us are starved for meaningful connection than ever, Rachel has put together a wealth of useful tips all of us can use to up our game when it comes to connecting and relating. Not only are her tips thoughtful for professional networking, but the many real examples she provides are useful tools for us to navigate connecting and networking in many different contexts in our own, authentic way."

—**Andrew Blotky**, author of *Honestly Speaking: How the Way We Communicate Transforms Leadership, Love, and Life*

"The thought of networking can paralyze, or it can catapult your career. You decide. In today's disconnected and fragmented business world, Simon teaches you 'the goods' on how authentic relationships (even virtually) can be your most powerful currency yet."

—**Paul Epstein**, former NFL and NBA business executive; bestselling author of *The Power of Playing Offense*

"*Relationships at Work* is a must-read for anyone who needs to navigate and thrive in any organization, whether it's a fast-growing start-up, a multinational, or something in between. Simon has done invaluable work here that so many people inside a company can use: new hires, mid-career folks, managers—and even executives. Her many examples of emails to write, situations to navigate, and checklists will help anyone who wants to succeed at their job (and really, life itself)."

—**Karen Wickre**, bestselling author of *Taking the Work Out of Networking*

"This is so much more than a book to help you approach networking with more ease and confidence—even as an introvert! This book is a practical guide to help you create, foster, and deepen meaningful and inclusive relationships at work so you can build a rewarding and results-driven career."

—**Kelli Thompson**, leadership coach, speaker, and author of *Closing the Confidence Gap*

RELATIONSHIPS AT WORK

HOW TO
Authentically
NETWORK
WITHIN
YOUR
COMPANY

www.amplifypublishing.com

Relationships at Work: How to Authentically Network within Your Company

For more information, please contact:
Amplify Publishing, an imprint of Amplify Publishing Group
620 Herndon Parkway, Suite 320
Herndon, VA 20170
info@amplifypublishing.com

Library of Congress Control Number: 2022920832

CPSIA Code: PRV0323A

ISBN-13: 978-1-63755-537-8

Printed in the United States

———————————

To Jason, who envelops me with happiness, support, and encouragement. I love the life we have built together.

———————————

RELATIONSHIPS
AT
WORK

HOW TO
Authentically
NETWORK
WITHIN
YOUR
COMPANY

RACHEL B. SIMON

amplify
an imprint of Amplify Publishing Group

CONTENTS

INTRODUCTION

My Networking Journey

magine you're about to walk into a large room of colleagues who you barely know. You hesitantly pause at the sign on the door marked Networking Event. You put on your name tag, take a deep breath, and cautiously enter. Your palms are sweaty, your heart is racing, and you sincerely don't want to be there at all. You make a mental list of all the excuses that would easily justify why you could turn around and leave from the mountain of work you need to accomplish to the fact that you simply don't like these types of events. Why force yourself to attend something you don't even enjoy? But you've heard that networking is important, so you walk in anyway, an excellent first step.

You quickly survey the room and find it to be just as intimidating as you'd feared. The attendees all appear to be enjoying themselves and look to be engaged in deep, meaningful conversations. You feel completely out of place, and your inner monologue is on overdrive, having a field day. You think to yourself, *What am I even doing here? How long do I need to stay? I'm an imposter, just playing the role of someone who belongs. I'm pretty sure everyone knows I'm an imposter. Wait. Does everyone know I'm an imposter, or is that in my mind? Oh my, I think everyone knows! Where's the door?* It takes every bit of energy to keep yourself from walking out, mere seconds after

1

you managed to walk in. Everyone, except you, seems to be skilled at this whole networking thing, and you wonder why you even bothered to come.

I'm there in the room too—a seasoned, accomplished executive at one of the world's largest corporations. I wonder if you can spot me. See that woman across the floor having a relaxed conversation with a small circle of strangers, effortlessly chatting with a twinkle in her eye? Um, that's not me. See that other woman seamlessly floating from group to group, warmly chatting and exchanging contact information? Nope, that's not me either. See the woman practically hugging the back wall, trying to blend into the wallpaper, and hoping that someone—anyone—will join her in that spot for a conversation? Yup, that's me.

It's true: I'd prefer to do just about anything than attend a large networking event. Or, what I refer to as an introvert's worst nightmare. People are often shocked to learn I'm an introvert, as they mistake being cheerful and friendly—I'm both!—with being an extrovert. But the definition of being an "introvert" lies with how I focus my thoughts inward to myself rather than outward to the world. It's how I draw my energy from within and prefer to recharge on my own rather than around others. Being around people for too much time drains me. Even though I fake-it-till-I-make-it with an outgoing smile because networking is essential and part of my job, it's still strenuous.

I was a shy child, and even as a young adult I generally kept to myself. I enjoyed hanging out with my loving parents, sisters, and a few close friends—OK, one close friend—and I didn't really feel the need for many more people in my life. Their companionship, encouragement, assistance, views, and opinions were enough. The idea of interacting with dozens—or hundreds!—of people I didn't know petrified me. What would I say? How would I connect? Not only did I not see the point of it all but it seemed so daunting. I was just fine in my small circle, in my tiny corner of the world.

Yet I decided to make my career at a large publicly traded corporation.

In all fairness, it wasn't enormous when I was initially recruited as a college graduate. But even at fifty thousand employees versus the over three hundred thousand it grew to at one point, I knew I wasn't exactly joining a mom-and-pop operation.

If I didn't see the point of networking as a child, I quickly learned the importance as soon as I embarked on my career. Much like eating my vegetables or exercising, it was one of those activities I detested but knew I needed to do for my own well-being. When I attended company networking events and conferences, however, not only did I marvel at the struggle it took just to coax my introverted self into showing up but I also noticed a pattern in which I never emerged with new contacts who could be helpful professionally or personally. I attended, checked the imaginary box that it was complete—I appreciate a good to-do list—and patted myself on the back for putting forth the grueling effort. Yet I always left with no definitive positive outcome. I was clearly going about networking all wrong.

In time, I took a different approach and said yes to happy hours and social events with my peers. I arrived with high expectations and a generous stack of business cards to hand out, as that's what I observed others do, but I struck out there too. Conversations felt forced and superficial, and I can't recall one single contact I developed at one of those large events that yielded a significant relationship. My experiences were neutral at best, even negative in several distinct situations in which I felt belittled and unimportant. Once again, networking was a losing proposition for me.

Nonetheless, ever the optimist, I tried another approach. I heard from several reputable sources that I should learn to play golf if I wanted to succeed in Corporate America and form a network within my company. I begrudgingly enrolled in lessons alongside a few colleagues and took the same class twice because I failed it the first time. Don't ask me how I couldn't manage to pass an extracurricular golf class that wasn't for a grade—I just know it was highly recommended to me by the instructor that I start all over again. Wow, not only did I loathe golf but I evidently wasn't even satisfactory at that either. Furthermore, I hadn't met anyone to network with during the process, as my initial classmates had the audacity to pass the first class and progress to advanced skills—show-offs! Oh, and I'm also very frugal, and golf was shaping up to be an expensive hobby. After I barely passed my second class, I never set foot on a golf course again.

Over the years I tried reading books written by networking experts, and while I highly respect the authors for sharing their experiences, very few resonated with me. Many were written for professionals who wanted to network *outside* their companies for new job opportunities or to gain new clients in their fields, such as real estate, financial counseling, or multilevel marketing. That wasn't what I was seeking. One book began with an anecdote of a successful businessman who made his first billion dollars by utilizing his college network. Gee, I just wanted to find the courage to ask a peer to have a cup of coffee with me! It seemed as though I was on my own to acquire these skills, and I began to wonder if there was a way to network simply by being myself. No golf, no business cards, no happy hours—just me and my authentic self.

That was the ultimate question: How could I network in a genuine manner, in a style that was true to my personality? I'm proud to say that after many years of starts and stops, through various failures, anxieties, embarrassments, and valuable lessons, I ultimately cracked the code on how to authentically network within my company. The best part of all is that I learned to relax and enjoy the process of developing meaningful relationships that have inspired, motivated, educated, and assisted me beyond my greatest hopes and expectations. These relationships have also propelled my career.

Just as the phrase "leaders are made, not born" applies to so many of us, please take comfort in the fact that strong networkers are made, not born, and I'm living proof! It's fair to say I didn't wake up this way. If you ask anyone in my circle of family or friends about my skills in this area when I was younger, I'm confident they would've voted me least likely to be an expert. In a twist no one saw coming, least of all me, I've gradually blossomed into the ideal person to share my experiences. I initially wasn't successful at networking, yet I found my way. And you can too.

Let me tell you about the origins of this book: Several years ago, I led a small mentoring circle of about a dozen employees, and during our first session I inquired about the topics they'd like to discuss. A résumé session? Absolutely. Interviewing skills? Of course. They asked for sessions on subjects for which I could easily lead. But among the common suggestions came an unexpected request. They asked, "Rachel, will you teach us how to network?" Well, that was an interesting proposal, and one I'd never considered. My answer was swift and emphatic: no.

Mind you, this request came exactly twenty years into my career, and over that time I had become quite successful at establishing and nurturing relationships. I had risen through the ranks from what my company refers to as a "first-line" manager, where I supervised frontline union-ized employees, to a "fifth-line" senior management, or vice-president, position. I'd earned increasing levels of responsibility, which included leading teams of thousands of employees, managing billions of dollars of revenue and expense, and executing large critical projects. I was respected by leaders who knew my strong work results, as well as those who knew of my collaborative style through my solid reputation. My success was primarily due to the network I had established, which I built one person at a time, one cup of coffee at a time, and one conversation at a time, through genuine interactions and authentic exchanges.

But how would I teach this to others? I suppose I was quite competent at networking and knew many remarkable colleagues who would drop everything to assist me. Yet I didn't know how to *explain* what made me effective in this area.

We went about our mentoring circle, and as promised we discussed preparing résumés to be in perfect shape and examined skills to ace an interview. But this group was very persistent. They frequently and playfully jabbed that if only they could learn about networking skills it would be the best circle they ever attended. Dang, they were convincing. I took the bait and rose to the challenge.

I sat down in a quiet space and created tips I could offer on how to network. One led to another and then to another and then to another, until I ultimately had penned a sizable list. I laid it out in a series of slides and accompanied each of my tips with a *real email* I had either sent to a colleague, or they had sent to me. I spent countless hours searching through my email folders, looking for the perfect illustrations to make the tips come to life. The emails were tangible, concrete, eye-opening examples of just how simple networking could be when done with sincerity, kindness, humor, and compassion.

I was nervous to give my presentation for the first time. I felt vulnerable as I offered all my advice in such a personal manner. After all, my inner thoughts, writing style, voice, and tone were all on full display. Would it be considered unprofessional that I sometimes write emails with smiley faces and exclamation marks? It turned out this made me appear down-to-earth. Would it make me look unsuccessful if I explained some of the pitfalls I've had with networking? Apparently, this made me relatable. Would my presentation still make networking seem so daunting? It had the opposite effect, as my plethora of examples demystified networking and empowered the audience to immediately put the suggestions into motion.

The presentation was met with resounding success. And if it's possible for an unrecorded speech to go viral, that's exactly what happened. I'm frequently asked to share this topic within my company, so often that I've given this presentation on average every four weeks since its inception. It's something I do with great enthusiasm, and I'm honored every time I'm asked to present. At this point, many people in the company have seen the presentation more than once, and they tell me they gain something new every single time they hear it.

What's really interesting is that the presentation seems to resonate with everyone: people who are just starting their careers and those who have been working for quite some time; people who are entry-level managers and those who are senior management; people who work at headquarters and those who work from home. In particular, introverts have hailed my presentation as a breakthrough in how they view and form connections. In this digital world, people want and need human relationships more than ever, and I provide a road map on how to make it happen.

Invariably, each time I deliver the presentation, I'm humbled when I hear, "Rachel, you should write a book." I've heard this for years, yet I had to give it a lot of consideration, as I wasn't sure the message would translate outside my company. It does.

I'm told the best part of my presentation is the real emails exchanged with my colleagues, which demonstrate just how easy and natural networking can be. When I present within my company, I use my coworkers' emails in their entirety to illustrate the tips, as it's a fun component for the audience to see names they recognize projected on the big screen. Although colleagues have granted permission to use their emails, for this book, I've opted to change names, clean up extraneous details, and at times merge a few emails, threads, and recollections into one to help move the narrative along. In addition to these illustrations, in each chapter, I offer a personal story about how I learned the tip, provide fresh examples, and propose questions to consider as you embark on your networking journey.

The most fascinating part of writing this book was the realization of how applicable my tips are for those who work from home. For many years, I ventured into the physical office every day—that is, until the COVID-19 pandemic forced us to reimagine how and where we work.

Out of necessity, I pivoted my own networking to a virtual environment and was pleased to discover that my relationship-building skills remained as authentic, effective, and solid as ever.

If you were in the audience during my presentation, I'd assign you homework. Yes, you read that right—homework! I'd instruct you to implement two of the tips we discussed and email me a month later to share what you accomplished. My goal is to keep the participants motivated to take the advice and convert them into action. For many, having an assignment gives them the courage they need to begin, which then yields the momentum to incorporate networking as a part of their regular routines. As a result, I have thousands of examples of how these tips have worked for thousands of people, many to their great delight and astonishment, and I'm confident you'll have the same success.

I'm thrilled to guide you in this process as you learn to authentically network within your company just by being yourself—really! Even if you don't work at headquarters. Even if you work from home. And especially if, like me, you're an introvert. Read on, and I'll show you how.

Why Is Networking Important?

Most of us would agree that networking within our companies is essential. Actually, I'll go out on a limb and state that virtually every reader of this book understands that it's critical—after all, you picked up this book for a reason. You know it's important and may want to improve your skills, but why?

Now, that's a very good question, especially for us introverts, who acknowledge that engaging other people, even ones we know quite well, might seem akin to having a root canal. So why do it?

I joined my large company directly after graduating from college with my business degree. I loved the company then and still do. The values, ideals, and aspirations have always appealed to me, and from day one I knew I wanted to make my whole career here. Several decades later, I have indeed done just that, a concept that is almost unheard of these days. I've consistently admired our leaders' vision to guide us through change. When I was a young professional, these executives seemed larger than life, with their charismatic personalities and keen business sense, and I learned many lessons by watching them. Now that I'm at the same level as many of the leaders I had revered, I'm acutely aware of how employees might be watching and learning from me. Therefore, I seek to lead with purpose, clarity, authenticity, and approachability.

With tens of thousands of employees, I've always considered our size to be simultaneously one of our biggest strengths and biggest weaknesses. To my freshly employed eye, the most significant drawback was that we sometimes operated in "silos," or self-contained environments. Interacting with colleagues outside the silo walls wasn't exactly the easiest or most natural thing to do. When I started my career, I worked in a sales call center in a Kansas City suburb, and I barely intermingled with managers in the other call centers across Kansas and Missouri, let alone leaders within different departments. We were a complex maze of dozens of organizations—engineering, human resources, corporate strategy, etc.—which served us well for throughput and productivity, but this model presented challenges for sharing ideas and collaboration.

There were a few people, however, who seemed to partner effortlessly across other organizations, and I studied them with heightened interest. Their networking skills appeared to boost them to a bright, sunny spotlight, where they reaped benefits of new job opportunities, promotions, and praise to a higher degree relative to their peers. Although it terrified me, and despite my insecurities and lack of confidence, there was a part of me who wanted to be like them with the hope that I, too, would earn opportunities to expand my skills and undertake new roles. But in reality, most people who networked were eyed with suspicion for their ulterior motives. Therefore, while I knew I needed to give networking a try, I also knew I needed to be cautious with my approach.

It dawned on me that the people who emitted a self-serving vibe gave networking a bad name. If I were to label these people, I would call them "the climbers." These coworkers seem only to be interested in climbing the corporate ladder and engaging in relationships when they can glean something from it for themselves. They appear to act differently around upper management than they do around others. It doesn't mean they aren't lovely people. Some of the nicest, most helpful people I've worked with over the years fall into this category. But they viewed work relationships differently than I did, and I could sense their styles a mile away. I knew that once our relationship had no more fruit to bear for their personal gain, it would be over. I never wanted to be viewed as a climber, since I actually consider myself to be the opposite. In fact, throughout my career, I never once thought I was ready for any of my promotions.

In my mind, I was at a crossroad. I saw colleagues who I viewed as networking experts veer in one direction, where they benefited from high-profile connections and opportunities to showcase their skills. Meanwhile, other disenchanted colleagues turned in the opposite direction and opted out of the entire networking process altogether. Many of them kept a low profile and remained in the same roles, in the same cubicles, for most of their careers. I knew it didn't have to be this way.

The biggest realization came from learning that networking is *not* about meeting someone who will give me my next job. Instead, networking is about developing relationships with mutual benefit, or sometimes, with absolutely no professional benefit at all. I frequently have people schedule time on my calendar to ask me how to get promoted. I patiently explain the paradigm shift that must occur to network in a genuine, authentic manner. The key is to build and nurture long-term relationships merely by being themselves. It takes effort, courage, thought, and time, but it's actually not difficult to do.

The bottom line is that if anyone would look at someone's actions and label them as "slick," "manipulative," or dare I say "slimy," they're doing it wrong.

Let's return to my initial question: Why exactly is networking important? Why even bother? Here are the seven reasons networking has become essential to me:

1. Networking breaks down my big company into "six degrees of separation." I'm referring to the Kevin Bacon game, in which the celebrity can be linked to any actor or actress in Hollywood within six interconnected points. It's the same within my company. I may not know who to call, but I know someone who knows someone who can assist me. There have been countless times when I begin an email by saying, "You may not be the right person to help me. If not, can you please point me in the right direction?" I'm appreciative when I have a reliable network in place to provide a warm handoff to another colleague. It's been critical to my success in getting work done expeditiously and efficiently.

2. Networking helps me get my job done easier, faster, and better. When I know who to reach out to for help or to answer a question, I'm able to cut right through the clutter and get things done quickly. Collaboration and partnership are essential because there's a certain risk of working in a vacuum that doesn't need to be taken. Having a network in place to share ideas and solutions helps me predict the unintended consequences of my actions and understand how my choices might affect other departments. When I bring in my network up front, I don't have to spend unnecessary time on the back end, justifying my decisions and smoothing things over, because I engaged the right people from the very beginning.

3. Networking allows me to meet people with diverse views and perspectives. The older and wiser I grow, the more important this aspect is to me. I'm not just referring to different opinions on policies or work-related issues but also life experiences, backgrounds, cultures, and perceptions. It may be comfortable and easy to surround myself with people who are just like me, but I've also learned the value of surrounding myself with people who are very different. I now have a

remarkably diverse network of people of all levels, ages, nationalities, races, religions, and job histories. These relationships not only aid me professionally but they also enrich my life.

4. Networking provides both parties with a boost of confidence. In fact, when done properly, networking makes people feel really good! I'm going to return to this point time and time again throughout this book. Actually, this phrase will be reiterated verbatim throughout every single tip to remind you of the power of authentic networking. I've learned the value of developing connections in a genuine manner, which means letting colleagues know when their leadership resonates with me or that I feel inspired by their actions. Who wouldn't want to hear that?

5. Networking allows me simultaneously to be a giver and a taker. I have a lot to learn, but I also have something to offer, which enables me to be both a great listener and a strong contributor to the conversation. I ask lots of questions, but I also chime in with my opinion. The best relationships are reciprocal.

6. Networking is vital because a fully developed network *now* might come in handy when I need it *later*. I love the book title by Harvey Mackay, *Dig Your Well before You're Thirsty*, as it sums up this very theory. Sometimes people hear me speak and lament that they hadn't learned this concept earlier in their careers. As the Chinese proverb says, "The best time to have planted a tree was twenty years ago. The second-best time is now."

7. And finally, networking *can* lead to new job opportunities. Please note the word "can" is italicized. I would put the word in neon flashy lights, if I could, to further drive home my point. Every lateral job I've rotated to and every promotion I've earned have occurred due to my network, but that's never been the focus of my actions. Having an array of colleagues who know my skills, talents, strengths, and

capabilities has unknowingly emerged as my most reliable asset. As a result, I've been tapped on the shoulder multiple times to assume new responsibilities by people who could vouch for my work ethic, grit, and abilities.

By now I hope you're convinced networking is important, and you're ready to dive in. Throughout this book, we'll explore twenty fundamental tips with over two hundred examples to authentically network within your company. I'm excited to share!

TIP 1

Introduce Yourself When You're New in a Job

For me, the hardest part of starting a new job isn't landing the job—it's actually *starting* the job. It doesn't matter my experience or how many years I've been with the company; I'm always nervous to take on something new. And yet I have in fact started many new positions. I've rotated throughout the company multiple times, sometimes after only eighteen months and other times after five or six years. I should note that I've never once been offered a role I've applied for internally within the company. Though we have a robust online job board, I've been 100 percent unsuccessful at getting *any* of the jobs I thought I wanted and believed I was qualified for. I was rejected from literally all of those—some after an apparently failed interview and others after I assumed my résumé didn't even make it past the human resources screener. Instead, I've always been tapped on the shoulder to take on a new position.

It's a pattern that has repeated itself many times over the years, when I'm contacted completely out of the blue and asked to take on a different role. I incredulously listen to the hiring manager, all the time wondering, *What on earth makes her think I can do this job?* Nope, I think to myself, *I like my current job, and I don't want to change.* An extreme lack of confidence begins to swirl inside my head, and I conclude that there's no possible way I can be successful in the position I'm being asked to take. Why would she even ask me? I want to put my head in the sand to hide.

Of course, my insecurities are hidden by my enthusiastic smile, and I always graciously accept the job. And guess what? Not only do I love the new role but I also excel at it.

A great quote by an unknown author says, "The comfort zone is a beautiful place, but nothing ever grows there." Oh, I love that! I've let this quotation guide me as I've anxiously embarked on new adventures. I've learned to thrive in a place of discomfort, and I've discovered ways to bloom where I've been planted.

But still, day one for me on anything, especially starting a new job, is the most challenging. Changing roles is tough. After all, I was usually a top performer in my last position, knew everyone, and had a tremendous ability to get things done. How would I replicate that, and quickly, in my new role?

In my early years, I kept a basic list, and whenever I came in contact with new colleagues, I would jot down their names and job functions. It was so useful, and I would often reference the simple spreadsheet when I became overwhelmed with a task. I would conduct a rapid scan of the document to see who could help me remove an obstacle, think differently about an issue, or point me in the right direction. In essence, who could help me to become unstuck when I didn't know what to do. It's interesting, because in hindsight, as a new employee, I never once thought of this as networking—I just thought of it as survival, since I was clueless!

Over time, the list grew quite long, and it was extraordinarily helpful, but it took me months and months to accumulate the names to put on it. I would often meet someone and say, "Ah, I wish I had met you eight months ago, when I was working on that critical project. I could've benefited from your wisdom then." I was glad to have met this person now, but *earlier* would have been super helpful. As I took on more responsibility and was expected to hit the ground running with high speed, I realized I needed to meet contacts sooner. I needed to be more intentional about meeting colleagues early in my new job to develop relationships *before* I needed them. I wondered what I could do to hasten the process. Essentially, all I really had to do was ask.

You see, I've learned to ask my new teammates who I need to have a relationship with to be successful at the very start, with an email like the one below:

From: Rachel Simon
To: Simon Direct Report Team
Subject: Hello Team!

Hello!
I'm delighted to be joining the finance organization. This is a top-notch team with such a great reputation! I'm truly happy to be here.

I've scheduled time with each of you this week for us to get to know one another. In addition, I'd like for you to consider who I need to have a relationship with beyond our team to be successful. Think about key partners and co-dependent organizations.

Thanks and I'm looking forward to working with you!
Rachel

These "hello" notes are met warmly—my new team members are typically pleased that I not only reach out so quickly but that I also give them an opportunity to be helpful to me so early on.

I usually receive a list of about ten people, and I write them each an individual email asking for some time to get to know them, like the following example:

From: Rachel Simon
To: Dave Tabber
Subject: Introduction

Hi Dave, I hope all is well with you.

As you may know, I have recently assumed Debbie's responsibilities in finance. I understand that our teams work closely together and I'd love to set up an introduction meeting.

I'll find a spot on our calendars to schedule some time. Thank you so much and I look forward to working with you.

Rachel

From: Dave Tabber
To: Rachel Simon
Subject: RE: Introduction

Sounds good, Rachel. Looking forward to it, and welcome to the team.

Dave

I really appreciated meeting Dave so early in my new role. He was gracious with his time as he explained his position and how our teams interacted. Not too long after our initial meeting, we found ourselves working on a complex project together. I was glad to know him beforehand, which accelerated the trust we had in each other.

Within days of starting my new role, I send introduction notes to the names I receive from my teammates. I also ask my supervisor for input during our first one-on-one meeting, and in turn I receive valuable recommendations; once this even included someone who had previously held the job, which was a fabulous connection. Although it's hectic and crazy to start a new job, I make these introductory meetings a top priority instead of putting them on the back burner for when things slow down. In reality, things don't slow down for quite a while, do they? I've discovered that it pays dividends to devote time to relationships *before I need them*. I like to think of it as investing in a rainy-day fund. I do this because the one thing I know for certain is that at some point it's destined to rain.

A few months after I started my new job, I reflected upon the relationships I had formed with my direct reports and the original names they had provided me. I then asked myself if there was anyone else who I should get to know. Of course, there were still plenty of people, so I asked my teammates, "Who else do I need to have a relationship with for our team to be successful?" After I received a refreshed list of names, I once again sent an individual email to another dozen colleagues.

From: Rachel Simon
To: Dan Fentley
Subject: Time on your calendar?

Hi Dan,
Now that I've been in my job for 90 days, I am ready to come up for air and learn more about our finance team.

I'd love to chat for 30 minutes and find out about the great work your team does, how our teams may interact, and just get to know you better. OK to schedule some time?

Thanks – looking forward to meeting with you!

Rachel

From: Dan Fentley
To: Rachel Simon
Subject: RE: Time on your calendar?

Absolutely. My assistant can help arrange a meeting. Thanks for reaching out.

Dan

It was invaluable to get to know Dan. When we met, he was one level higher than me, and as time progressed he was promoted again to an extremely large and influential role within the company. I'm grateful for the strong relationship we formed, which I can trace all the way back to this introductory email.

This tip is also useful for establishing relationships with peers who share the same supervisor. My friend, Tia, once lamented to me that she didn't know her coworkers very well, as they were scattered across the globe, and they didn't partner together on any issues. Except for awkward greetings on conference calls once a month, they rarely interacted. I encouraged her to reach out to them, as they could be helpful in learning the ropes, establishing comradery, and gaining insights. I shared an example of an email I had sent to my peer Wendy when I joined the team:

From: Rachel Simon
To: Wendy Looper
Subject: Hello!

Hi Wendy,
I'm very excited to be joining Jamie's organization! Mind if I schedule some time in the next week or so to connect? I've heard great things about you and would love to learn about what's on your plate and what you're responsible for. I'd also appreciate any insights about the team, top priorities and how to quickly add value! ☺ Thanks so much!
Rachel

From: Wendy Looper
To: Rachel Simon
Subject: RE: Hello!

Welcome!
I'd love to find time to chat. In the meantime, if there is anything you need or anything with which I can help, please let me know. Looking forward to working together.
Wendy

I sent a similar note to all nine of my coworkers, who also reported to my boss. I increased my knowledge about the team's culture and norms that would have taken weeks or months to unfold in the regular course of business. Tia really appreciated this tip, and even though she was not new in her role, she sent a note to her colleagues to get to know them. She knew she was on the right track when she received an enthusiastic and immediate reply expressing that the feeling of isolation may be mutual.

From: Tia Shinani
To: Kwame Badhu
Subject: Hello from the US to South Africa!

Hello Kwame,
We have been on the same team now for over a year (isn't our boss the best?). We rarely interact beyond the staff calls, yet I find the work you do very intriguing. Are you OK if I schedule a video chat for us to connect? I know you have three teenagers like I do, and it would be fascinating to compare the differences and similarities of raising our kids in different countries.

If this sounds good, I will get it scheduled for us. Looking forward to it.

Tia

From: Kwame Badhu
To: Tia Shinani
Subject: RE: Hello from the US to South Africa!

Hello Tia, what a fantastic idea. I often feel a bit disconnected working in another country and I would welcome the conversation. My calendar is up to date and we can find a mutual time zone that works for both of us. Thank you for reaching out.

Kwame

Let me validate your thoughts right now that sending these emails can be a bit scary. Actually, a lot scary. What will the recipients think? Will they respond? In almost every single case, I receive messages back saying yes to an introduction and welcoming me to the team. Every now and then, I don't receive a response, and that's all right. I just move on, and I certainly don't take it personally. Occasionally, I receive a message back saying, "Shame on me, I should have been the one to reach out to you!" Why yes, yes they should have. We'll discuss how to welcome others to the team in tip 16.

A special note for supervisors of large teams: Dig deep into your organizations to get to know your team members. I'd like to assume most leaders immediately prioritize getting to know direct reports and understand the importance of ensuring employees with a new boss feel secure, valued, and appreciated. Paranoia can run high in the workplace when a new leader takes the reins, so whatever we can do to ease concerns goes a long way. In that spirit, I encourage you to make it a priority to form relationships with employees several layers down. The time it takes to invest in each person is rewarding and builds mutual trust. When I joined a new team, I sent this note to the direct reports of my direct reports and was transparent in what I wanted to discuss.

From: Rachel Simon
To: Simon Director Team
Subject: Introduction 1x1s

Hello Director Team! I've scheduled time with each of you individually over the next two months and I'm looking forward to getting to know you.

Do not prepare a formal presentation, but please come prepared to discuss:
1. Tell me about yourself personally and your job responsibilities.
2. What has gone well this year? What accomplishments are you proud of? What have been your challenges? What can I help with?
3. What is your goal for self-development? What are you working on to be a better manager and leader?

Thanks so much – I am excited to connect and learn more about you!

Rachel

How would you feel if your department's new leader scheduled time to get to know you? I expect you'd be excited and impressed that she took an interest in meeting her new colleagues. *Remember: when done properly, networking makes people feel really good.* I'm going to reiterate that point over and over again throughout this book. Reaching out to others not only benefits your ability to succeed in the workplace but it also serves to create mutual feelings of trust and value in the process.

READY TO TRY?

Here are some sample emails to get your creative juices flowing. Edit them to fit your own writing style and unique situation.

From: You!
To: Sally Jones
Subject: Introduction

Hi Sally,
As you may have heard, I've recently joined the human resources organization and understand that our teams are partnering together on a special project. I'd love to set up 30 minutes to get to know you and learn about the responsibilities your team manages. If that sounds good, I'll look at our calendars to find a good time.

Thanks – looking forward to meeting with you.

From: You!
To: Tyrone Nelson
Subject: Hello from a new colleague

Hi Tyrone,
I'm thrilled to have joined our company. When I asked around about who would be a good person to get to know, your name kept coming up. Can we grab a cup of coffee one day?

Thanks!

From: You!
To: Maria Alvarado
Subject: Looking forward to working with you!

Hi Maria,
I recently joined the marketing department after spending the last seven years in the public relations organization. I am excited to be here, to learn, and to add value. I've seen your name on many reports but we haven't had the chance to meet in person yet. Would you mind if I schedule some time for us to get to know each other?

From: You!
To: Chantall Quinn
Subject: Consolidation project

Hi Chantall,
I joined the conference call this morning when you gave an update on the consolidation project. You did a really nice job explaining it. I'm new to my position and I've been working to get up to speed on a topic I know little about... I have to say yours was the best, clearest read-out I've heard yet!

Would you mind if I schedule a few minutes to chat about your overall role? I suspect I have a lot to learn from you. Thanks so much.

If you're not new in a position, you can send an email like the examples below:

From: You!
To: Harriet Adams
Subject: Hi there

Hello Harriet,
It's hard to believe I've been in my role for as long as I have without formally reaching out to get to know you...OK if I schedule 30 minutes on your calendar? I'd like to learn more about you and discuss the big project we're working on together!

From: You!
To: Rick Beasley
Subject: Get together

Hello Rick,
I'd love to learn more about what your team does. Although we see each other virtually at various meetings, we've never sat down to talk one-on-one. If that sounds OK, I'll get a virtual session scheduled for us. Thank you!

QUESTIONS TO HELP YOU GET STARTED

- Who do you need to form a relationship with when you start a new role? Are your peers who share the same supervisor a good place to start?
- How will you identify additional relationships you need to form? Will you ask your boss, peers, or direct reports?

- How many people will you reach out to? When will you aim to have that complete?
- How will you keep track of the people you meet and their responsibilities? Will a simple spreadsheet or contact list do?
- If you lead large teams, how will you meet your colleagues several layers down?
- What other communication tools does your company utilize besides email that you could leverage to introduce yourself? Think about social media platforms, messengers, apps, etc.
- Who hired you for your role? Did you participate in a panel or group interview? Should you reach out to them for suggestions?
- If you aren't new to your role, should you take the time to utilize the same strategies?

TIP 2

Follow Up with Contacts You Make

One thing that completely exasperates me is when people complain there's no opportunity for "fill in the blank"—no opportunity for exposure, no opportunity for promotion, no opportunity to try new assignments, and so on and so forth. I especially cringe when they say there is no opportunity to meet people to network with as though they are waiting for a bright neon sign to flash "Networking opportunity! Hear ye, hear ye! Step right up!"

Even when structured networking opportunities are available, many people sit them out. They often hide behind the excuses of too much work, not enough time, or that they simply need to rearrange their pencil collections. Hey, I pass no judgment, as structured networking events are perhaps my least favorite activity to do. Still, these are often the same people who grumble that there are limited opportunities to stretch themselves with a new position.

My colleague Rick says, "There is opportunity everywhere." That's an insightful comment on so many levels, and one of the most profound statements I've ever heard, since it applies to all areas of our lives. There are ample opportunities to shine in our jobs, plug gaps, step up, and create something out of nothing.

Because networking relationships have meant everything to me as I progressed through my career, I watch for circumstances for them to develop organically. I've already shared that every job I've had within my company has come about from a networking relationship, both lateral roles and promotions. But I also credit my relationships with simply getting my work done.

We meet people all the time in the course of our day, but how often do we seize the occasion to follow up and form a connection?

I was at a large event when I met Tili. During our conversation, she mentioned she had just been in a car accident and was pretty sure the woman who hit her was texting and driving. For context, this was at a point in time when distracted driving was emerging as a significant safety issue, and we agreed we were passionate about bringing attention to the topic. I spontaneously exclaimed, "Oh, you need to send her a 'Texting and Driving—It Can Wait' sticker!" We both laughed at the thought of sending this to a complete stranger who had just crashed her car, so imagine my surprise when I received this email from Tili the following day:

From: Tili Meeker
To: Rachel Simon
Subject: Thank you

Hi Rachel,
At the Women of Finance event yesterday, you encouraged me to send a "Texting and Driving – It Can Wait" sticker to the driver that rear-ended my vehicle recently. I am happy to report that I wrote her a note today and the mail, including the sticker, is on its way.

You gave me the "nudge" that I needed to take action and I wanted to thank you for that. It feels good to help spread the message and get more people involved in this great cause.

Thanks again and have a great day. ☺
Tili

I was delighted to receive her email. Not only was it thoughtful and quite funny—can you envision the woman's face when she opened that envelope?—but I learned a lot about Tili through this one note. She is bold, passionate about topical social issues, immediately follows through with ideas, and is proactive about closing the loop. Her email made me feel valued, as if our conversation spurred something positive to happen in the universe. *Remember: when done properly, networking makes people feel really good.*

A few years ago, I met Tiffany at a training class. It was a three-day-long course, and over that period I met about one hundred people. I sent the email below, but only to five colleagues I either sat next to or had a conversation with during a meal.

From: Rachel Simon
To: Tiffany Botts
Subject: Great to meet you in training!

Tiffany,
I just wanted to drop you a note to tell you how terrific it was to meet you in training this week. I enjoyed your insights and your can-do personality!

If I can ever help you in the areas of payroll, accounts payable, or sales comp (or if you have ideas on how we can make things more effortless), please don't hesitate to reach out.

Rachel

If I had sent that email to all one hundred people I had met, it would've come off as insincere and pretentious. But the five people I sent it to were specific colleagues with whom I wanted to keep in touch. Sure enough, not long after our email exchange, Tiffany had a question that she knew I'd be able to answer. Later, I had an inquiry I knew she could help with. My follow-up email after our initial meeting was the perfect link to place us in each other's networks.

I met Kara while at lunch at a local deli. I was in line, ready to make my purchase, when another colleague introduced us. We said hello, exchanged a few pleasantries, and then went our separate ways to eat our healthy salads. OK, I had a Reuben sandwich. With chips. At least they were baked chips. When I returned to my desk, I received an invitation from Kara to connect on our company's social media site.

From: Kara Melton
To: Rachel Simon
Subject: You are invited to join my network

Hi Rachel,
It was a nice surprise to meet you while having lunch today at the deli with Danielle. I'd like to add you to my social media connections.
Kara

> From: Rachel Simon
> To: Kara Melton
> Subject: RE: You are invited to join my network
>
> Thanks Kara, it was lovely to meet you as well. Let's connect soon!
> *Rachel*

I marveled at how quickly Kara set this into motion, and I readily accepted the invitation. As with Tili, I learned a lot about her through this one exchange—she takes the initiative, uses company tools like our internal social media platform, and is looking to expand her network. I was also impressed that she added a note about where we met rather than just sending a blind invitation. What's noteworthy is that our relationship blossomed into a mentoring relationship, and it all started with us meeting at the cash register—where I'd like to point out I did turn down a chocolate chip cookie, thank you very much—and she followed up that very day. Ask yourself how many times you might have let this opportunity slip away when someone introduced you at lunch, in the elevator, in the lobby, or even in a virtual meeting, and then you went your separate ways? How remarkable that Kara used this opportunity to form a relationship.

I met Jan at another training class. It was a small session in which we participated in group projects and team competitions to apply our knowledge; therefore I got to know Jan well over the course of a few days. We shared a lot of laughs and enjoyed each other's company. During the span of the training class, I received a call offering me a new job as the chief of staff for one of our most senior executives, Ray. I had known him for years, but once again it surprised me to be tapped on the shoulder for a new job. I accepted the role and started just a few days later. Imagine my delight when I received the following email:

From: Jan Carlton
To: Rachel Simon
Subject: Checking in...

Hi Rachel!
I've thought about you a couple of times this week wondering how the new job is going! Hope it's going well and you are enjoying it!

Jan

From: Rachel Simon
To: Jan Carlton
Subject: RE: Checking in...

Hi Jan! That's so nice of you to check in. It has been phenomenal! I'm already loving this job and have learned more in the past 4 days than I have in years – literally. I feel so wide eyed like "I can't believe I'm here!" ☺

I really want to get together for lunch – I'll get a date on the calendar. Thanks for checking in!

Rachel

The email from Jan was incredibly thoughtful. We had just met in the training class, something eventful happened in my career with a new job offer, and she took the time to follow up. It made me feel special and kicked off a lasting friendship.

I'm often asked about social media platforms—how I use them and if I find them to be effective for networking. My answer has evolved over the years from an emphatic "No, I'm not even on social media," which I acknowledge sounded remarkably out of touch and had a "get off my lawn" vibe, to a current "Why, yes, I'm on LinkedIn and have found it to be very useful," which I acknowledge doesn't make me sound hip, but at least it makes me sound current. Since the focus of this book is about networking *within* your company, I won't spend a lot of time detailing how I've used the site to form connections with colleagues at other companies; indeed, I've used LinkedIn to connect with contemporaries after I've heard them speak on a webinar or after I've met them at a conference. There are a plethora of authors and LinkedIn experts you may want to seek out if you think this angle would be helpful in your networking journey. Yet LinkedIn has also deepened relationships with many of my internal connections. It has been enlightening to read their posts about how they see the world and how they connect various topics to their jobs. We support each other through "likes" and comments, and I encourage you to do these two actions in tandem—click the "like" *and* also leave a comment. You will stand out among others as a supporter by taking a few extra seconds to personalize your interaction rather than simply using the emoji buttons. For example, I posted this comment to Anne after a poignant post on MLK's birthday:

Rachel Simon
Vice President

It will indeed take all of us to make MLK's dream a reality. I am so inspired by your passion and most of all, your action. You are making a meaningful change every day with the way you lead your team and community!

In tip 6, I'll outline the many ways I reach out to colleagues during holidays and special milestones. LinkedIn does make this rather easy with pop-up reminders, so I'll often use the site to express my well-wishes.

Rachel Simon
Vice President

Larry, congrats on your service anniversary! I'm so appreciative of our relationship and am grateful for all of your wisdom and advice. I'm looking forward to many more years of working together! I hope you know just how valued you are on our team.

If LinkedIn is a tool you personally use to connect, grow, and nurture relationships, I would love to connect with you there! You can find me at https://www.linkedin.com/in/rachel-b-simon-ab306a18b/.

READY TO TRY?

Here are some sample emails to get your creative juices flowing. Edit them to fit your own writing style and unique situation.

From: You!
To: Dorona Levine
Subject: Great to meet you!

Hi Dorona,
It was so nice to meet you yesterday at the collaboration meeting. You were sitting next to Margie, who was kind enough to make an introduction. I have heard so many great things about you and would love to get to know you better. Would you mind if I schedule some time on your calendar?

From: You!
To: Nitesh Ahuja
Subject: Follow up from earlier today

Hello Nitesh,
We were both on the virtual roundtable conference call today and you made a comment about diversity and inclusion that really spoke to me. I think we have a lot in common. I work in New Mexico and you're in Florida – would you mind if I schedule a virtual coffee for us? I have a few ideas on how we can advance this discussion and would love to get your viewpoint.

From: You!
To: Omar Lopez
Subject: Follow up from earlier today

Hi Omar,
We sat next to each other in the Town Hall earlier today. You said you work in the customer insights group and it occurred to me that's a fascinating area of the business that I know nothing about. Would you be open to grabbing a cup of coffee one day to chat?

You

From: You!
To: Lisa Kitchens
Subject: Hi there

Hi Lisa,
We met in the lobby earlier today when Kayla introduced us. It was great to put a face with the name after all of these years! I work in the legal department so please let me know if I can ever assist you!

Of course, sending a note immediately after you meet someone may be best, as it says something about your personality and your follow-through. But what if you met someone a while back? Is it still OK to follow up? Absolutely! There is no statute of limitations on how long it could be to reach out in the world-according-to-Rachel. If you consider it from the receiving end, would you be offended if you received a note several months later, like the one below, or would you feel great that this person recollected your name when thinking about such a positive topic?

From: You!
To: Quinn Potter
Subject: Hello

Hi Quinn,
We met several months ago at the sales kickoff and I have been meaning to reach out. I enjoyed hearing your thoughts on employee engagement – you seem to have a lot of success at motivating your team and I'd love to pick your brain! Would you mind if I schedule 30 minutes for us to reconnect?

You

QUESTIONS TO HELP YOU GET STARTED

- Who did you interact with—whether at a meeting, an event, or merely a greeting—who you'd like to get to know better?
- Who did you meet recently with whom you should follow up? Challenge yourself to make a list each week of new people you came in contact with for the first time and then send a note.
- Do you readily take advantage of the natural networking opportunities all around you in meetings and your workplace? Can you sit next to someone new at meetings?
- Did someone make a comment on a conference call or video meeting that resonated with you? Can you reach out to get to know them better through a virtual coffee?
- Is there someone you met a while ago who you'd like to reach out to, realizing it's never too late?
- Can you utilize social media—using your company's internal platform, if applicable, or an external site, like LinkedIn—to identify areas you have in common before reaching out? This may help you craft your introductory note.

TIP 3

Arrange Lunch or Coffee (In Person or Virtual)

I read a thought-provoking book many years ago by networking expert Keith Ferrazzi, titled *Never Eat Alone*, and you don't need to read it, because the title kind of says it all. I'm joking—you should pick it up! It's a terrific book, and the author had a strong influence on me. I took away many wise nuggets, the biggest and most obvious being that since I must eat anyway, I may as well eat with others. Brilliant!

Believe it or not, even with my hectic and full schedule, I have coffee or lunch with someone just about *every single day*. On days I'm in the office, it's in person; and on days I'm working from home, it's virtual. And I've discovered they are equally effective.

When I first joined the company, I consistently ate lunch by myself. Because I worked in a call center environment, we were required to spread our breaks over several hours to ensure management coverage. I would slip away for an hour, most likely to a drive-thru to eat in my car and listen to the radio. As much as I liked my coworkers, it never even occurred to me to ask someone to join me, as it was neither the culture nor the tradition of our small office. A short time later, I found myself working in a large headquarters setting, and while it wasn't corporate headquarters, it was similar, with a few thousand people in a downtown multibuilding complex. The department I joined was a close-knit team of about fifteen people, and I noticed right off the bat that everyone appeared to enjoy each other. It seemed as though they'd worked together for years, but in reality it was a newly formed group that was just beginning to bond. Still, they knew each other relatively well, and I was envious of their warm connections. The week I arrived, new to the scene, and with my fresh observations of how well they worked together, I prepared to head to lunch by myself as usual. Instead, I sent an email to the team, asking if anyone wanted to join me, and I was surprised when almost everyone said yes. What started as a get-to-know-you lunch for the newcomer turned into a daily meet-by-the-elevator-at-eleven-thirty-if-you-want-to-go ritual. There were different combinations of the group that attended due to inevitable conflicts, but I joined practically every day. If I was on vacation, the lunches often didn't happen. The meals were nothing fancy, as some people picked up food from the cafeteria, while others brought leftovers from home. In fact, I cannot recall a time we ate at an actual restaurant, although we must have, because there were a dozen eateries within walking distance. On nice days, at my request, we would eat at a picnic table outside the building, and I must confess that my definition of a "nice day" in Texas was ninety degrees. These sweet colleagues must have *really* liked me to indulge me by eating outside in this type of heat! Sometimes members of our leadership team walked by as we ate, playfully calling us crazy to wilt in the heat together and remarking on our group's closeness. These lunches made me extraordinarily happy, and it was a time in my career when I flourished professionally and personally.

How on earth did shy little Rachel become the social lunchtime coordinator, something that would have seemed inconceivable just a few short years before? It's not really a question of how, rather of why. Just as the *Never Eat Alone* author suggests, I needed to eat anyway, so

I figured I should eat with other people. Better yet, I should consider eating with people who may be able to help me. The lunches not only aided me in building strong friendships—many of these colleagues were at my wedding—but they also helped me succeed in my position. The first jobs of my career were very leadership-based positions, as I worked with teams in call centers. It wasn't rocket science in any way, and though I made more than my fair share of mistakes, nothing was irreparable. I was able to learn by observing others to do things better the next time a particular situation arose. But this new position was very different, as it was a policy role in which I established rules, methods, and procedures for a new area of the business. If I made an error with an ill-conceived policy, the consequences could be severe and impactful for years to come. I was afraid of making poor decisions, since I was such a novice; therefore I decided to seek many opinions on a subject before I brought forth a pro- posed policy to my supervisor. That's where these lunches became useful. I couldn't pop into my colleagues' cubicles fifty times a day to ask questions. I would've been viewed as someone who couldn't make a decision on her own, or worse, annoying. Likely both! But the lunches were perfect. They were excellent for building comradery and also provided the safety net I desperately required. As we talked about our personal lives, hobbies, and families, I would also ask questions regarding the policies my colleagues were tackling, such as, "How did you come to that conclusion?"; "What were the unintended consequences?"; and "What else did you consider?" I was a student eager to learn from them—not only the decisions they made but also the processes they used to arrive at a conclusion. They unknowingly saved me from several painful blunders, and I was grateful for the comfortable way in which I was able to accumulate my knowledge.

I've carried the lesson about the importance of eating lunch with my colleagues throughout my career. The group lunches served me well during that particular time period, but they have since evolved primarily to one-on-one-meals or coffees with coworkers of all types. This is how I've built my network with meaningful connections—one person at a time, one lunch or coffee at a time, and one conversation at a time.

Who exactly do I eat with? Early on, my scope was very narrow, as evidenced by the fact that I went to lunch only with people in close proximity, mostly peers with whom I shared the same supervisor. I didn't even venture to the other side of the floor to form relationships, let alone the other side of the building or—heavens, no—another department! Now my lunches and coffees consist of people from all organizations, of all levels, and of all backgrounds.

If I were to show an illustrative snapshot of my calendar for five days, lunches and coffees would look something like this:

- **Monday:** Corey—I met him the first year I joined the company, when we were both first-line managers. He became a senior leader in human resources, and we have remained close for decades.
- **Tuesday:** Isabelle—She was an attorney when I worked in California. She came to Dallas, so we scheduled lunch, and it was terrific to catch up.
- **Wednesday:** Mike—He was my supervisor for many years, and he promoted me twice. We had countless mentoring conversations.
- **Thursday:** Lori—We worked together on some complex projects, and it was important that we had a good relationship in order to be aligned and on the same page.
- **Friday:** Sunela—We met at an event when she was a second-level manager in finance. She asked me to go to lunch, and we established a relationship.

My calendar looks similar to this all week long, all month long, all year long. I go to lunch or coffee with just as many people from the departments

I work in as I do from other groups. I go with just as many people higher up the chain of command as I do with colleagues with lower levels of responsibility. I go with just as many people who have been with the company for decades as I do with new employees. I go with people from different backgrounds, races, religions, ethnicities, and countries of origin. I'm proud of how diverse my network is, and I consistently gain new perspectives.

There are a zillion reasons why you may think this tip is not for you. I've likely heard every roadblock and obstacle out there. I've identified ten of the most common explanations (excuses?) of why people say they can't do this tip —if these are your reasons below, let me dispel them for you with examples of how to make it work! I want you to understand this concept really is for you, as face-to-face human contact over a meal or beverage—in person and virtual—is one of the primary ways I've built a robust network.

1. *I'm on a budget, and eating out is expensive.* That's a fair point, to which I firmly say, "Stay on your budget!" Remember: you don't have to spend extra money to put this tip in motion, as you don't have to go *out* to lunch. You can go to the cafeteria, the break room, or another common area in your workplace. You can bring your own leftovers or a brown-bag lunch. Or you can do it virtually, a suggestion I'll repeat more than a few times throughout this chapter.

Also, please note if you think you neither have the time nor the budget to eat out every day, you don't have to go out to eat *every day*. Go once a week, once a month, once a quarter, whatever fits your life. If you bring your lunch from home, consider having someone join you to eat as illustrated in the email below:

From: Rachel Simon
To: Sam Bennett
Subject: Lunch today?

Hi Sam,
It looks like a gorgeous day! I brought my lunch from home and plan to sit outside enjoying some sunshine. Want to join me around noon? Let me know!
Rachel

I've also found that venturing out for coffee can be less expensive than going out to lunch. Although, I must say, my favorite coffee—a nonfat, decaf, no whip, no foam mocha—is not exactly a frugal drink!

2. *I don't have time to take a break, so I just eat at my workspace.* Many of us could say this, and there are times I have to eat at my workspace as well, buried in critical work. Those of us whose companies conduct business in multiple time zones often find ourselves with a lunchtime meeting. When this happens too often, I need to make a conscious effort to schedule lunch when I spot an opening.

From: Rachel Simon
To: Adithi Patel
Subject: Lunch break tomorrow

Hello Adithi,
I realized I've eaten lunch at my desk the last few days, which is not making me happy. ☺ I'm pretty sure that you're in the same boat since we've been on many of the same conference calls! Tomorrow's call is over at noon and I plan to actually go out to the local deli. Care to join me? It'd be great to get to know you better!
Rachel

If you consistently have meetings over lunchtime, perhaps coffee meetings are a better way to go, as they can be done at any time of the day. A colleague shared that she's been able to successfully employ this suggestion by arranging a midmorning or late-afternoon break. Since she is responsible for driving her children to school in the morning, she can't meet during times that most peers have their first dose of caffeine. Yet they all take her up on her offer for an odd-timed break; she just needed to ask. That was an ingenious way to make face-to-face time work for her schedule. I also find that coffee meetings are shorter—I typically schedule them for thirty minutes, whereas lunch meetings are usually sixty minutes. And if the coffee meeting is held virtually, it's even more of a time-saver, as I don't have to build in the walking time to or from the coffee shop.

3. *I work from home and wish I could have coffee with a colleague, but she lives in a different city thousands of miles away.* Technology is amazing—use it! There are countless technologies—Zoom, Cisco WebEx, FaceTime, and Microsoft Teams, to name a few—that make it seem as though my colleagues and I are sitting in the same room.

From: Rachel Simon
To: Vanessa Sherman
Subject: Virtual coffee?

Hi Vanessa,
I was thinking the other day how much I enjoy working with you and how I wish we lived closer so we could have coffee together. You are always such a ray of sunshine on our conference calls! Then I realized we could still have a virtual coffee. Want to meet for a video session one day next week. BYOC (coffee) of course. I'd love to get your perspective on the big project we've got going on and just get to know you better. Sound good? If so, I'll get that scheduled for us!

Rachel

If it seems scary to send a note like this to a peer, consider how you would feel on the receiving end. I bet you would feel delighted and may stand a little taller knowing that you've made an impression on a coworker. *Remember: when done properly, networking makes people feel really good.*

I've consistently used this tip over the years to enjoy virtual coffee with colleagues located all over the world—I partook in virtual coffees before virtual coffees were cool. It became even more practical when I began working from home, and had to pivot all my in-person coffees to be held via video. Did I miss the cozy coffee-shop feel? Absolutely. Did I miss the handcrafted mochas? Yup. Did I miss the coffee-shop prices? Um, no. With our cameras on, the conversations remained as warm and genuine as if we were sitting across the table from one another.

4. *This tip would be easy to put into motion if I worked at corporate head-quarters.* To this, I would raise my eyebrows and say, "Oh really?" because I put this tip into motion even when I worked in a small billing call center in Wichita, Kansas, which was hardly a bustling headquarters city for my company. Once I arrived, having earned my first promotion, I arranged lunch with the woman who ran the sales call center. I also scheduled lunch with colleagues from external affairs, regulatory, and other departments. There were plenty of people to go to lunch with; I just needed to expand my idea of who to invite, as there was only one peer from my own department. Within my large company, I'm confident that at least fifty-two people live in every major US city so that an employee could go to lunch with someone new once a week for a whole year—without repeating the same person twice. Perhaps that's your situation.

From: Rachel Simon
To: Shaniqua Masters
Subject: Hello from a Wichita colleague

Hi Shaniqua,
I've been in Wichita for about five months now and would like to meet more people in the area. I run the billing call center downtown. I understand you lead the external affairs team which sounds interesting. Can we meet for lunch one day? I'm flexible with my schedule and can come to your location. If that sounds good, I'll get something scheduled for us.

Thanks – I look forward to meeting you!
Rachel

And, of course, with virtual coffees as an option, there is absolutely no reason to feel limited by the fact you may not work at corporate headquarters.

5. *I'm an introvert and go to lunch with the same close friend every day.* This is an excellent start, as you're not eating alone, and I have a valuable suggestion to expand your circle: A few years ago, I started a series in which I schedule lunch with a peer I'm close with, and then we each invite someone to join us who the other person doesn't know. It's an introvert's dream since it's a group lunch, but with the security of a BWFF (best work friend forever) who I know really well to keep the conversation going. I've met scores of people this way who I would've never met if I had just waited for our paths to naturally cross.

From: Rachel Simon
To: Kandi Jameson
Subject: Lunch

Hi Kandi,
I've started a series with my peer Maggie where we go to lunch once a month and each invite someone we think the other person doesn't know. I've met so many people this way and I think you'd enjoy it. We have our next one planned for October 1 and you are my pick this month. ☺ Can you make it? Let me know!

Rachel

You can also easily implement this idea in a virtual environment. If you and your BWFF both work from home, you can easily conduct a video session with multiple people and have the same outcome as an in-person lunch.

6. *I don't like individual lunches and prefer to go out in groups.* Group lunches can definitely be a great idea if you're new to networking and worried about carrying a conversation on your own the whole time. Team lunches are a comfortable place to start with people in your own department who share the same supervisor. You can also go to lunch with several of your former colleagues from a prior department. If an in-person meeting ends right before lunchtime, you can spontaneously ask if folks would like to grab a bite to eat. Alternatively, think about groups of people you have something in common with, such as the group of women I organized in the email below:

From: Rachel Simon
To: Sue Bloom
Subject: What do you think of this idea?

Hi Sue,
I'm thinking of organizing a quarterly lunch for female colleagues who have school-age kids. We're all in the same season of life, doing our best to balance our careers with our growing families. We can think of it as a support luncheon... or group therapy, whichever term you prefer. ☺ I attached a list of local women who I think fall into this category – anyone else we should add?

I'm excited about our first lunch!

Rachel

7. *I want so much more than superficial lunches and want to form deep, meaningful relationships.* For those of you who really want to break down barriers and learn about your colleagues' backgrounds, I created an initiative called DINE!, which stands for Discover Differences, Include One Another, Navigate New Perspectives, Eat! This initiative started as a result of a call to action by my company's former CEO to move from tolerance to understanding. He encouraged us to dig deep to get to know our colleagues and learn about our backgrounds, experiences, sacrifices, and what makes us unique. I was inspired by his speech but didn't quite know how to put it into motion. One day, while perusing social media, I came across a meme that read: "A Christian, a Muslim, a Jew, and an Atheist all walk into a coffee shop. And they talk and laugh and drink coffee and become very good friends. It's not a joke. Honestly, it's what happens when you're not a jerk." Ah, this meme was the inspiration I needed and spurred the next step. The following day at work, I invited five people to lunch who were different than me. The lunch was incredibly successful, as we actively listened to each other's

stories. At its conclusion, I asked the participants if they would host their own lunches with other colleagues. They did, and a movement was born. DINE! has since spread across my company as well as to other companies. You can find out more at www.dolunchdifferently. com. This concept works equally well in a virtual environment. Of course, in that situation, it's a DIN rather than a DINE (no eating!).

From: Rachel Simon
To: Fabricio Perez
Subject: An invitation to DINE!

Hi Fabricio,
I recently heard about a grassroots initiative focused on diversity and inclusion. It's called DINE! which stands for:
> Discover differences
> Include one another
> Navigate new perspectives
> Eat!

I believe it is more important than ever to discuss diversity, challenge our own biases, and get to know each others' stories. I believe many people want to...they just don't know how to engage in these sensitive conversations. The concept of DINE! is that I will organize a one-time, small lunch with just 4-5 other people where I will invite people who are different from me (different in any way...race, religion, gender, background, culture, upbringing...). At lunch, we will openly share our backgrounds and the lens through which we view life. This is casual, everyone pays for themselves, and a great way to network and learn about each other on a deeper level.

I really like this idea, so I'm going to organize a DINE! lunch and I am inviting you to be part of it.

If this lunch sounds good to you, I will look for a date that works for all invited guests. I am looking forward to a great conversation – and perhaps everyone at the lunch will be inspired to host a similar DINE! event as well to keep the grassroots initiative going!

Rachel

---

8. *I am anxious about who will pay the bill if I initiate the lunch.* Who pays the bill when I go to lunch with a colleague? It's situational; for instance, if I invite someone to say thank you for a job well done, I'll definitely pay. At times I'll pick up the bill if I'm a higher level than the other person, although there are no rules around this. But the majority of the time we split the bill, regardless of who initiated the meeting. If you think you'd be worried the whole time about who's paying—*Oh my, he ordered lobster and caviar and thinks I'm picking up the tab?*—then my suggestion would be to choose the type of restaurant or coffee shop where you each order and pay individually at the counter rather than waiting for a bill to arrive at the table. And if you're anxious about the possibility of your invitation being misinterpreted that you're treating, when that's not your intention, then invite someone to a brown-bag lunch, go to the cafeteria and go through the line separately, or meet for coffee, which would likely be less expensive than lunch. Or, of course, you eliminate this anxiety completely if you plan the coffee or lunch to be virtual.

9. *I don't drink coffee.* OK, fair enough—not everyone loves coffee as much as I do, so please feel free to substitute "coffee" for any beverage of your choice. One of my colleagues doesn't drink coffee, but she always has a sparkling water in her hand, so I sent her the following note:

From:	Rachel Simon
To:	Eliza Samuels
Subject:	Topo Chico Break? ☺

Hi Eliza,
How about a break in the café one day next week – I'll bring my coffee and you bring your beloved Topo?

Rachel

You can easily invite someone to a nondescript "beverage break"—if it fits your company's social norms, this could even include an adult beverage during happy hour.

10. *I have no idea what to talk about at lunch or coffee.* Hold that thought! I have all sorts of ideas and recommendations to help you have a productive and meaningful conversation in tip 7. I promise we'll get there in just a bit.

I hope I accurately depicted all your reasons you might have for not sharing a meal or beverage with a colleague. If you bring forth additional justifications, I'm sure I could dispel those as well. The bottom line is that we're all busy, and we can all make legitimate excuses for why this tip isn't practical. But since you need to eat anyway, aim to never eat alone.

READY TO TRY?

Here are some sample emails to get your creative juices flowing. Edit them to fit your own writing style and unique situation.

From: You!
To: Diana Greenberg
Subject: Lunch this week?

Hi Diana,
I'm making a goal to eat lunch less at my desk and to go out at least once a week with a peer. It seems lofty but I'm up for it! ☺ Would you like to grab lunch with me one day this week? I'm available either Tuesday or Thursday at noon. Let me know!

You

From: You!
To: Anthony Jewel
Subject: Virtual coffee?

Hi Anthony,
I've enjoyed working from home in my current position, but miss having coffee and lunch with colleagues. Then I realized why not have a virtual coffee? It would be great to connect and catch up since it's been a while. Mind if I schedule one for us via video? Thanks!

From: You!
To: Molly Armstrong
Subject: Hello from a fellow Virginian!

Hi Molly,
We've never met but I was looking through the company directory for who else may live in the area since I'm so far from company headquarters. I love the flexibility of being a full time telecommuter but I admit I miss the in person interaction.

I was delighted to find there are several of us in the area so I thought I'd reach out to say hello and see if you'd like to meet up one day for lunch. I work in the billing department and I see you work in customer care – I'm sure we know many of the same people and our work may even overlap.

Would you like to meet for lunch one day? I look forward to meeting you!

From: You!
To: Trent Lexington
Subject: New restaurant – want to try?

Hi Trent,
There's a new Mediterranean restaurant that just opened up down the street and I remember you telling me how much you like this kind of cuisine. It would be great to get to know you better outside of the capital planning meetings we attend together. If that sounds good, I'll schedule something on our calendars!

From: You!
To: Winston Morewood
Subject: Coffee break?

Hi Winston,
It's been seemingly impossible for me to schedule lunch with people I want to get to know better (you), so coffee it is! Want to join me for a coffee break at 3PM tomorrow or Thursday? If you're working from home, we can do it virtually as well. I'd really like to tap into your expertise about the project we're working on together.

Let me know if that works for you!

QUESTIONS TO HELP YOU GET STARTED

- Who is someone in your department you can invite to lunch, either in person or virtually?
- Who do you interact with in meetings with whom you'd like to improve the relationship over lunch or coffee?

- Do you have time in your schedule and money in your budget for lunch? Should you invite someone to coffee instead, or should you meet up for a brown-bag lunch? Would virtually work better in your schedule?
- If you work from home, who else lives in your city who you could get to know? Do you have a company directory you could utilize to see who else is local?
- Which technology should you use to schedule a virtual coffee or lunch?
- Are there groups of people with something in common you'd like to assemble for lunch?
- Is the atmosphere at the restaurant you've selected conducive to a conversation so you can easily talk?
- Do you need to be aware of any dietary restrictions before proposing a restaurant, such as a vegetarian menu? If you're nervous about this, should you wait for the other person to suggest a place first?
- Where will you meet your colleague, such as in the lobby, at your desk, at the restaurant, etc.? Be sure to include logistic details in the calendar invitation.

TIP 4

Join Something

I wasn't born to be a joiner. Some people are naturally wired to be around other humans and to seek comradery. For them, if life is an ice cream sundae, then participating with other people is the cherry on top. At times I really do envy extroverts. They look at colorful advertisements for upcoming club meetings and events and wonder how they will choose. Can they do more than one? They *all* look amazing and life changing! Some people love to join for the experience itself, while others participate because of FOMO, or the fear of missing out. I don't have a shred of FOMO and don't experience regret passing on an event. I'm just not a joiner by nature, which is why I have to push my introverted self to be one.

I attended the University of Texas with fifty thousand other students, enrolling without knowing a single soul or stepping foot on campus, yet excited about a fresh beginning. The first weekend I enthusiastically partook in an outing to the Barton Springs swimming pool but had a cruddy time because I didn't even remotely like the people I was with. Another night I attended a party and felt overwhelmed trying to connect with students I had nothing in common with, a skill I wouldn't develop until many years later. I was fairly shy in my classes, and the few people I introduced myself to didn't pan into friendships. The days turned into weeks, and although my first semester at school wasn't completely miserable, since I did make friends with a few of the young women on my dorm floor—one of whom remains one of my dearest friends to this day—I floundered. That's really the best word—I didn't drown, but I didn't thrive. I wasn't unhappy, but neither was I fulfilled. I was just. . . there. Perhaps you know the feeling. I didn't know how to meet people with whom I shared common ground as a base to grow a friendship. Then, one winter day, while strolling to class in the business school, a flyer caught my eye for a professional women's business organization. I convinced myself to be brave and attend. Walking in by myself was difficult—remember from tip 1 that starting day one is always the hardest for me. I almost walked out seconds after I walked in. But it was the best decision I made during my years in Austin. The smart women I met that night were open and welcoming, and I signed up to be a member on the spot. Over the next three and a half years, not only did I form my closest friendships and have the invigorating college experience I was eager to have but I also assumed leadership roles and learned valuable lessons that I carried forward. Joining that organization was the missing puzzle piece, as it suddenly took that big school of fifty thousand students and shrunk it down to one hundred accessible students. Meeting people and nurturing friendships became so much easier.

It's a formula I've repeated many times in my life. When I wanted to form relationships at my kids' elementary school, I joined the Parent/Teacher/Student Organization. When I wanted to build relationships as they entered high school, I joined the Engineering Booster Club board. When I wanted to create relationships at my synagogue, I joined a few committees. I may not be a natural joiner, but as an introvert I've learned the importance of finding, building, and sustaining connections. I feel so much more confident walking in someplace where I know other people and where I'm respected for my contributions. For me, the best way to do that is to become involved.

It's the same within my company. When I was hired, there were about fifty thousand employees, and I should note I thought at the time that was *huge*. A few decades later, the company grew exponentially, with employees all over the world. How would I meet people? How would I connect with colleagues beyond my own department? I knew what I needed to do: join something.

When I first started working, employee groups (EGs) were just taking off and since then have exploded with popularity. If you aren't familiar with them, EGs are groups of employees who share a common interest or background that cuts across the culture of a company, sort of like professional clubs. These might include organizations based on race, sexuality, gender, age, specialization, and more. At my company, membership is open to everyone, as the importance of allies is understood and valued.

If your company has clubs or groups like the EGs I described, the first step is to seek one out and join. The next step is to attend a meeting *in person* if you're geographically able to do so. If you're afraid to go by yourself, ask a colleague to go along, as I did in the example below:

From:	Rachel Simon
To:	Amy Checker
Subject:	Upcoming EG Education Session

Hi Amy,
I just joined an Employee Group for professional females. The featured speaker looks very interesting and I'm eager to hear her remarks – I attached the flyer. I really want to attend. Would you like to go with me?

Rachel

I'm glad I asked Amy to go along with me, which got my introverted self there, and I didn't have to walk in alone—perhaps that's a necessity for you as well. But I also encourage you to be brave and meet someone new once you arrive. As I outline in tip 15, make a goal to meet just *one* new person. If you tell yourself you need to meet five new people, you might not follow through. But meeting one new person? That's not so intimidating. Sit next to someone new and ask him what he does for the company. Engage him in conversation and implement all the tips I've provided to maintain the connection. Send him an email when you get back to your workspace to say you enjoyed your chat and that you'd love to meet for coffee one day to continue the conversation. You will likely make his day by following up and showing genuine interest—I know this to be true because I've put this tip into action many times over the years with great success.

Joining and attending meetings are excellent steps. Becoming an involved member is next to get to know and authentically network with the people you meet. We have a multitude of EGs, and they all offer a variety of events designed to hear education speakers, serve the community, raise money for student scholarships, and learn new work skills. There are countless opportunities to get involved in a multitude of ways. One of my favorite aspects of the EGs at my company is the mentoring circles they assemble, which are small groups of individuals—generally six to twelve—who meet once a month to explore various topics. During my career, I've participated as both a member and a leader. As I shared in my introduction, in the circles I host, we discuss such themes as résumé writing, interviewing skills, and—you guessed it!—networking. We also hold several sessions in which everyone collaboratively shares on such topics as the best advice they've ever received, their favorite TED talks, and more. The circles are composed of colleagues of all levels, ages, and backgrounds. It's a rewarding experience, but only to the extent that people actively participate, soak up knowledge, and vulnerably share their hard-earned wisdom. My mentoring circles are all held virtually on video, allowing for geographic diversity.

Employees join mentoring circles for many reasons, and I'd like to assume one of the reasons is to meet new people. Therefore, it continually surprises me when participants don't take advantage of the intimate structure, as it's an easy opportunity for like-minded people just waiting for one person to make the first move. Be that first person! Kit, a member of one of my circles, copied me on this email she sent to Jarod after the first session:

From: Kit Hampton
To: Jarod Hollis
CC: Rachel Simon
Subject: Hi there

Hi Jarod, when you gave your introduction today in our first mentoring circle meeting, I realized you're a person I'd like to get to know better. I have a strong desire to move my career toward a more technical focus and I think you'd have a great perspective since you've made that pivot.

We are both in Dallas - can we get together one day to talk?

Kit

From: Jarod Hollis
To: Kit Hampton
CC: Rachel Simon
Subject: RE: Hi there

Kit, I'm glad my passion for my career came across during my introduction. I'd be delighted to share the path I've taken including some lessons/tips I've learned along the way. Let's go to lunch.

And I learned from your intro that you're a Cal alum – Go Bears!

Jarod

Kit told me she sent a similar note to three other people in the circle. Just like that, she had new colleagues in her network who didn't exist the day before.

It's important not to limit your networking within the group to peers, as the circle *leader* is a valuable person to network with as well. After our initial meeting, I received the following email from Anna, a circle participant:

From: Anna Bigly
To: Rachel Simon
Subject: Thank you for your influential mentoring session

Hello Rachel, I wanted to thank you for your tips, ideas, and personal stories you shared with us during the first mentoring meeting yesterday. I was happy to notice I could relate to most of them (i.e. have a positive attitude, be yourself, don't just talk about problems, but propose solutions, etc.).

I am looking forward to learning as much as possible from our future mentoring circle sessions, and I will push myself to apply new ideas in my daily life to make a difference. Thank you for everything.

Anna

There are many things I love about Anna's email, especially the title. As I scrolled through my inbox, deciding which complicated issue to tackle first, this one popped out, thanking me for my "influential" mentoring session. Of course, I opened it right away! She was specific in her thank-you note about what she had learned. Out of ten participants in the circle, she was the only one to send me a note after that session. I had poured a lot of time, thought, and energy into the first meeting, and she took the opportunity to thank me. How do you think this note made me feel? *Remember: when done properly, networking makes people feel really good.* At the next session, I was looking for her, as she was the only person I knew at that point, based solely on our exchange. It gave her a leg up with exposure, simply because she took the time to send a note.

I was once asked the question by a participant of why I choose to lead mentoring circles. After considerable reflection, I concluded it's because I expect a return on my investment. If I'm going to commit time and passion into these sessions, I hope the participants emerge more knowledgeable, optimistic, and ready to soar. There were about a dozen people who heard me give this explanation, yet imagine my surprise when I received the following email from Rachael a few days later titled "Return on Investment":

From: Rachael Barch
To: Rachel Simon
Subject: Return on Investment

Rachel,
I want you to know I take to heart what you say every day and that your investment isn't lost on me. I'm appreciative of your time, and I summarized some of the ways you've made an impact and how I'm paying it forward.

- Networking connections – I've reached out to everyone in the circle and found common themes. Some have provided insight into challenges I face
- Training committee – I've gotten involved in the employee engagement committee to have maximum impact on everyone around me
- Fundraising for storm victims – being on this committee has been fulfilling and has inspired me to do more to embrace opportunities to help others
- Mentoring – I've tried to think about everything I've learned and how I can share it with fellow team members and people I supervise

I hope this makes your day in that your efforts are valued! ☺

Rachael

Wow! What an encouraging note. Yes, it did make my day. This doesn't feel like networking, yet it is. Rachael went out of her way to form a personal connection with me that paid dividends down the road when she needed advice and support.

My current department has many ways to get involved and meet new people. We have committees for diversity and inclusion, employee engagement, and culture. We have book clubs and movie clubs. We have opportunities to walk together for the American Heart Association and bowl together for Junior Achievement. All these options have virtual components, so it would simply be impossible to say there are no opportunities to meet people.

What if your company doesn't have anything like this? What if you don't have EGs, clubs, or mentoring circles? I have a crazy piece of advice for you: start one.

Yes, you read that right—start one. Someone has to, so why not you?

There are many low-risk, low-effort ways to do this. You could start a walking club in which coworkers meet to get in some steps during the day while they talk. You could initiate a lunch-and-learn series, in which colleagues bring their own brown-bag lunches and discuss a particular topic or listen to a speaker. You could organize an event for your fellow team members to participate in a community service day together. Some organizations have a built-in infrastructure, just waiting for companies to invite them in, like Toastmasters, a public-speaking organization. Before you embark, know your company culture well enough to determine if you should first obtain the approval of your supervisor or human resources partner.

Or you can go big as I did. On the first day that I started my first vice-president role within finance, I anxiously attended a senior management meeting with all my new peers. I gazed around the room and noticed there were approximately forty people in leadership positions and exactly six women, including me. I know there were six women because I counted them. I'm not sure how many females I was expecting, but surely it was more than six. I already knew four of them from previous jobs where our paths had crossed, but I quickly befriended a new face, Kathy, who had just recently been promoted as well. Over coffee, she asked if I had noticed the lack of women at the table. She wondered if we should do something about it and form an organization that would provide opportunities for women to shine.

I'm sure you can imagine every single thought that simultaneously darted through my head. I'm not a natural joiner; was I suddenly going to be a *starter*? I was on week one of an enormous new job; was I going to launch a new club from scratch? The leadership team barely knew my name; is this what I wanted to be known for before they even knew me for my management results? Would top leadership approve this? Did I even have time for this? There were a million reasons to say no. Instead, I gave an immediate and unequivocal *yes*.

Once Kathy and I locked arms with purpose and gusto, we engaged the other four women in leadership, and the Women of Finance was born. Within a few years of its launch, it boasted several thousand members. We created a robust organization for women—and men—to thrive, grow, and gain exposure. We focused on education, mentoring, and networking. As a founding member, you can be certain that networking would be one of the three pillars of our mission! I beam with pride whenever I think about what we built. Not bad for someone who doesn't like to join anything, right?

READY TO TRY?

Are you ready to give this tip a try? Here are some sample emails to get your creative juices flowing. Edit them to fit your own writing style and unique situation.

From: You!
To: Melba Catalones
Subject: Walking Club?

Hi Melba,
Our walk today got me thinking... want to start a walking club at the company? This would give us a chance to meet others and share ideas while we walk. I can send out an email and also post something in the breakroom. We can start small, like every Thursday and see where it goes from there. What do you think?

From: You!
To: Human Resources Leader
Subject: Mentoring Circle?

Hello Human Resources Leader,
If you aren't the right person to assist, perhaps you can point me in the right direction?

I understand that many companies have set up mentoring circles for employees who are interested in development and education. Is this something our company offers? I'd love to participate in one. If we don't currently offer this, is it something we can consider? I'd be happy to be on a committee to research and/or pilot one. Thank you so much for the consideration.

From: You!
To: Peter Crondell
Subject: Today's Professional Meeting

Hi Peter,
I attended the EG meeting today for Professionals Over 50. Thank you for organizing such a terrific speaker event – I got a lot out of listening to the presenter, especially about the concept of authenticity. You are doing an outstanding job as Education Chair for the group – bravo!

I would love to connect further and see how I can get involved on next year's board or on a committee.

Mind if I set up some time to discuss?

From: You!
To: Bailey Fanning
Subject: Seeking to serve the community!

Hi Bailey,
I'm looking for opportunities to serve our community. I understand that non-profits reach out through your team to request volunteers or board members. Will you please keep me in mind if you hear of an opportunity that fits my skillset and passions (these include animals, children and education)? Thanks.

From: You!
To: Annalise Beeker
Subject: Volunteer Day?

Hi Boss!
What would you think if we organized a community service day as a team? I volunteered at the local food bank last weekend and saw the need they have for volunteers, especially on weekdays.

I'm excited about this and think our team members would enjoy doing something to get to know one another outside the office. If this sounds OK, I can coordinate among our local team members and send out a sign up sheet. I have some ideas on how we can engage our international colleagues as well. Let me know your thoughts!

From: You!
To: Marco Gonzales
Subject: Meeting on Wednesday

Hi Marco,
I haven't participated in an employee group before and I'm nervous to attend on my own. There is a meeting next week – would you like to attend with me? I've heard great things about the group and I think we'd both enjoy it.

Let me know if you'd like to attend with me – thanks!
You

QUESTIONS TO HELP YOU GET STARTED

- Are there existing organizations, such as employee groups or clubs, at your company? Is there one in particular for which you would like to attend the next meeting?
- Does your company publicize or post opportunities for connections like clubs? How can you find out what is available?
- Is there a mentoring circle you can join? If you're already a participant, have you made an effort to connect with other members and the circle leader?
- If there are no organizations, can you start one? What are some ideas you have, ranging from low-risk, low-effort to high-risk, high-effort endeavors? Who is in a position of influence to help you successfully put this in motion? Do you need to chat with your supervisor or human resources partner?
- Does your company participate in a charitable giving campaign each year? If yes, should you consider joining the planning or fundraising committee?
- Does your company organize recognition, social, or spirit events? Is this an opportunity to get involved to meet new people?
- Can you ask a few of your coworkers to start a book club of relevant leadership and business books?
- Does your team enjoy potlucks or themed lunches? Can you work with others to form a committee to plan them on a regular basis?

TIP 5

Network through Your Network

A young woman attended my networking presentation for the second time in the span of one year. After it was over, she came up to thank me and asked, "Rachel, how are you so effective at networking?" I tilted my head to the side, looked at her incredulously, and asked if the advice I'd provided hadn't just answered that very question. After all, I'd spent ninety minutes outlining all the tips I personally put into practice. Did I poorly explain it, not just once but twice? She laughed and replied that yes, she loved the presentation, but she was seeking more insight. Why do colleagues respond to me so well? She had incorporated many of the tips into her daily work life but wasn't getting the positive response that she had hoped to receive. She pressed on—it's one thing to *ask* someone to go to lunch, yet it's another thing for them to *accept*. Furthermore, it's another thing for them to agree *again* and build momentum toward a meaningful relationship. She clarified the essence of her question: What personal characteristics do I possess that has led me to be successful at creating and nurturing a reciprocal and fulfilling network?

Ah, that's a fair question, one I needed to spend some quiet time to contemplate the answer.

What *does* cause someone to accept my invitation to lunch a first, third, or twentieth time? What causes someone to tap me on the shoulder for a new job? What causes someone to drop what they're doing to connect me with a colleague who can assist with my issue? What causes someone to do me a favor for which there is nothing in it for them? Why am I successful at networking, and moreover, how can I describe it in a way that is repeatable for others?

After careful consideration—that may or may not have occurred over a box of chocolates—I realized it comes down to this: I'm easy to work with.

Ta-da! Groundbreaking information, right? I realized a long time ago that I don't have to be the most intelligent or the most charismatic person in the company—for sure, some individuals run circles around me with those attributes. I don't have to hold the highest position. Even though I'm a senior manager, I developed a strong network long before I held that title. I don't have to be the most persistent—those people can often be obnoxious, and that's not an admirable quality! I simply try to be easy to work with. I show up to meetings prepared, get done what I say I'm going to do, and search for solutions to get to a yes rather than automatically saying no. I promptly answer emails, seek to understand others' diverse points of view, and project enthusiasm for the task at hand.

I appreciate people who are easy to work with, so I strive to be that exact type of person. I never want to be the coworker who hoards information or maintains an icy relationship during challenging times. When colleagues learn we will collaborate on a committee or a project, I hope their noses don't wrinkle up in distaste. Instead, my goal is for their eyes to light up, knowing I'll be a great partner. Similarly, when I invite someone to lunch or coffee, I hope they look forward to it with delight, knowing that I'll be both interested *and* interesting and that we'll have a mutually beneficial experience.

It wasn't always this way. My early years certainly saw their share of successes and failures, and if I'm honest, there was probably a broad spectrum of how easy I was to work with. While many relationships were solid, others were shaky. Some associations were cooperative, while others were slightly too competitive. Initially, I often sought to be right rather than to be a collaborative partner. I'm grateful for the gifts of experience, wisdom, and reflection, which have caused my leadership style to evolve tremendously over the years. I've soaked up feedback from mentors and supervisors who have generously coached me to a greater understanding of the big picture. I've learned to accept feedback without becoming defensive and to proactively ask for specific ways I can lead, manage, and perform better. This hard work—change is not easy!—has paid dividends toward my growth as an easy-to-work-with-colleague.

With this in mind, I've built my network for years often without even realizing it. Perhaps that's the position you're in too. A lot of my networking has occurred without putting a significant focus on it. As you're reading the tips in this book, you may be thinking, *Yes, I do that already*! and you may feel terrific about your progress. If that's you, keep up the great momentum!

But maybe this is also you: About midway through my career, I had a realization I needed to do more. I needed to move from subconscious to conscious networking, from low degrees of effort to increased activity. It occurred to me that many people in my network had either retired or were on the cusp of retirement. I needed to meet more colleagues, especially those in "a position of influence." I use that term loosely and broadly, because *influence* is neither defined by level nor by title. I previously shared that I've been tapped on the shoulder for every job I've taken within the company, for both lateral moves and promotions, and I realized I needed more people in my circle who could potentially do the tapping in the future. I needed to make a more mindful effort to build my network of coworkers who could learn about my talents, capabilities, interests, and passions. And how exactly was I going to do this? Just as I'd always done it—one person at a time, one cup of coffee at a time, and one conversation at a time, but this time a bit more intentionally.

I began this part of my networking journey by reaching out to someone who I knew and admired from afar. Debbie and I knew each other's names and had a vague familiarity with one another, but nothing more. I sent her the following note:

> From: Rachel Simon
> To: Debbie Stoughton
> Subject: Time on your calendar?
>
> Hi Debbie,
> It was good to see you yesterday at the Employee Giving luncheon! Congratulations on your new role – I'd love to learn more about what you're doing now in the customer care organization and how our teams may work together. Do you mind if I schedule some time on your calendar?
> *Rachel*

It was the type of note I send often, and there was certainly nothing unique about it. It's what happened *during* the meeting that provides the essence of this tip.

My meeting with Debbie was outstanding, and we had the kind of connection I wish I had with everyone. We talked about our career paths and our personal lives, and the time flew by. With such a great rapport, my next step would typically have been to ask if we could meet again in a few months. Instead, I posed a different question. I asked, "If you were me and wanted to learn more about some other departments in the company, who would you talk to?" She instantly replied that she would talk to Bob, who managed a large department. I courageously continued by asking, "Would you mind facilitating an introduction?"

Six words. Six brave words—that's all it took to get my network moving again. Those six words are the magic ingredients of this tip: confidently and graciously ask the person you're meeting with if she would mind introducing you to someone new.

Not only did Debbie reply, "Yes," but she stood up from where we were sitting, walked over to her keyboard, and typed the following email on the spot! Before I had even returned to my desk, Bob had replied.

From: Debbie Stoughton
To: Bob O'Connell
CC: Rachel Simon
Subject: Introduction

Bob, I just met with a delightful colleague who is energetic, passionate about leading large teams, and very sharp. You'd really enjoy meeting with her so I thought I'd make the introduction.

Debbie

> From: Bob O'Connell
> To: Debbie Stoughton
> CC: Rachel Simon
> Subject: RE: Introduction
>
> Thanks Debbie.
> Rachel, I'd be happy to meet! If Debbie thinks highly of you, you're definitely someone I'd like to meet. Please find a slot on my calendar.
>
> *Bob*

Just like that, I had a new networking meeting to schedule, and this began a fantastic domino effect. I met with Bob, had an engaging conversation, and ended with the same request I had made of Debbie. I boldly asked, "If you were me and wanted to learn more about some other departments in the company, who would you talk to?" Once he shared a new name, I asked once again, "Would you mind facilitating an introduction?" I continued this snowball meeting new people of all levels, in various departments, and of many diverse backgrounds and perspectives. It has been a gift that has kept giving.

Simply put, I networked through my network.

Asking for an introduction is the secret sauce of this tip. Every now and then, the request is met with, "Nah, you've got it on your own"—in other words, they don't want to do it—but overwhelmingly the answer is they'd be happy to assist. The warm introduction is important because it cuts through all the clutter and makes it super easy to reach out to someone new. Think about how different the reply might have been from Bob if I had emailed out of the blue to say, "Debbie mentioned you'd be someone good to talk with...". I doubt I would have received the same encouraging and immediate reply.

I gladly make this type of sincere introduction for others when they ask me for contacts. Below is an example in which I introduced Jamie to Brad.

From: Rachel Simon
To: Brad Dillinger and Jamie Swarza
Subject: Introduction Brad/Jamie

Hi Brad,

I'd like to introduce you to Jamie Swarza. She is new to the company – she joined the auditing department about 18 months ago. We have established a relationship and she is eager to expand her network, meet more people, and learn about future opportunities. I have found her to be smart, optimistic, curious and excited to be here. I think you'd be a great person for her to meet to explain what your team does and the path your career has taken. Would you mind if she schedules a meeting with you to get to know you?

I'll leave it to the two of you to connect! Have a great weekend.

Rachel

Brad was more than happy to meet with Jamie, and I ran into them having coffee together. It makes me happy to be a connector because I know how important relationships have been to me. Once, before a big senior manager conference, I asked a colleague who was new to the company due to a merger if there was anyone in particular she wanted to meet. She appreciatively explained that she really wanted to get to know more people in marketing. I kept an eye out for her and provided introductions when the opportunity arose.

Sometimes networking through your network can quickly get you to the right place or the right person with minimal effort. For example, I received this email from a fellow leader who passed along the name of someone interested in helping create the Women of Finance when we were in the early ideation mode:

From: Brooks Meyers
To: Rachel Simon
Subject: FWD: Thank you!

Rachel, yesterday I met with some new hires for a brown bag lunch to discuss career development. We have a couple of women who are part of the group and they're enthusiastic about the concept of a "Women of Finance" organization and are more than willing to pitch in. I've forwarded the note of one of the women who came up to me afterward.

Brooks

From: Ayesha Hosain
To: Brooks Meyers
Subject: Thank you!

Brooks, thank you for having lunch with the new-hires today. It was very interesting to hear about your career and your advice about moving from job to job. I'm excited about the idea of "Women in Finance" – please let me know if there is anything I can do to help get it started!

Ayesha

So Ayesha met Brooks, expressed her interest in helping, and Brooks directed her to me. We ended up tapping Ayesha to be on our founding board of directors for the new employee group. The way she got on our radar was by sending a thank-you note to someone in her network, who then sent her my direction for consideration. She networked through her network.

Another example comes from my former supervisor asking if I'd be willing to meet with someone with whom she had a mentoring relationship:

From: Sharon Danu
To: Rachel Simon
Subject: Favor

Rachel, I don't know if you remember Betsy Sanburg or not. She used to be in our group when you were on our team. She set up some time with me here in Chicago for some mentoring. She seems to be struggling with a plan to guide her career.

You are the best career manager and goal setter I know. I was wondering if you wouldn't mind meeting with Betsy over the phone for a half hour to talk about what types of things you did to manage your career and put yourself in a place where there were opportunities for advancement.

I gave her some suggestions but think it would be beneficial to talk with you. OK to send her your way?

Sharon

I admit I laughed out loud when I read the part about being the best career manager and goal setter she knows. My career has taken so many twists and turns, and not one of them was planned. It's quite interesting that she perceives me as being effective at proactively managing my career! But I digress.

The real point of the email is how Betsy was able to network through her network. She met with Sharon in Chicago, and then Sharon turned around and sent her my way via a warm introduction. Of course, I was more than happy to meet with her. We talked several times over the phone, and once Betsy moved to Dallas, our relationship continued to develop over lunch.

A further example is how I first met Daria when a colleague from another department sent the following email:

From: Charlotte Banier
To: Rachel Simon
Subject: Summer Intern

Rachel,
I have a summer intern who is amazing. She is smart and energetic and has added immediate value to our team. We will be sad when Daria leaves us in August.

She is working on her MBA and I thought she could benefit from a session with you since you are in finance. Do you mind if I make an introduction?

Charlotte

Naturally, I was glad to meet with Daria, who I quickly learned was just as talented as Charlotte described. I had a lovely lunch with her before she ended her summer internship. A year later I received an email once again from Daria, telling me that she had finished her degree and had been hired full-time by the company. She asked if I was open to having another lunch. Of course! I was touched that Charlotte thought of me to represent finance with an introduction, and I was impressed when Daria continued the relationship. Rather than being a burden or just another item on my to-do-list, I was delighted. *Remember: when done properly, networking makes people feel really good!*

You may also want to consider proactively offering to make connections, such as this email I sent to a new intern at our company:

From: Rachel Simon
To: Ari Ziegler
Subject: Would you like me to make any introductions for you?

Hi Ari,

It was great to meet you yesterday – I'm so glad you are with our company as an intern this summer! Is there anyone you'd like me to introduce you to while you're here? For instance, I know you are have an interest in political science, so I'd be glad to do a warm introduction for you to someone in our Washington DC office.

Let me know if you'd like me to do this (and any other departments as well). Summer internships are such prime opportunities to meet new people and help clarify what you'd like to do once you graduate, so I'm happy to help!

Rachel

Ari happily took me up on this and made the most of his summer internship. I consistently offer to make connections for newcomers, and the majority follow through with a short list of people they'd like to meet. Sometimes it's hard for people to ask for this kind of help—since I have a strong network, it is truly a pleasure to offer to make connections. And it's quite fulfilling when I see one of those connections develop into a job opportunity, mentoring relationship, or friendship—I feel like a company matchmaker of sorts!

READY TO TRY?

Are you ready to give this tip a try? Here are some sample emails to get your creative juices flowing. Edit them to fit your own writing style and unique situation.

From: You!
To: Octavia Realdo
Subject: A request!

Hello Octavia,
You've always been so gracious in offering help and I usually can't think of anything to ask of you. But now I do have a request! I'm interested in expanding my network here in the company. If you were me and wanted to meet more people, who would you encourage me to have a conversation with?

I'd love it if you would introduce me to someone new – it doesn't matter the department or the level – I'm just interested in meeting new people.

Thoughts? THANK YOU!

From: You!
To: Arthur Brewster
Subject: Contacts in your former department?

Hello Arthur,
I want to thank you once again for taking a chance by hiring me – it's hard to believe I've been with the company for eight months now! You've been an amazing supervisor and I've learned so much from you. Your mentoring and guidance have been spot on.

I'd like to expand my network and meet some new people. Before you were in marketing, you shared that you worked in client relations. Would you mind introducing me to one/some of your former colleagues? Thanks for the consideration!

From: You!
To: Christian Monterrey
Subject: Introduction to Gina?

Hi Christian,
It was great to see you in the coffee shop earlier today – I'm glad you're doing well! You were waiting for Gina from real estate to join you and it got me thinking that I'd welcome the chance to talk with her. I've always been interested in that part of the business and she seems great. Would you mind making an introduction? I'd be so appreciative!

Thank you – you're the best!
You

From: You!
To: Shiu-Yuen Cheng
Subject: Hong Kong Discussion

Hi Shiu-Yuen, I have a fabulous trip to Hong Kong coming up. I know your wife grew up there – do you mind asking her if I can call to get some tips? I appreciate it!
You

From: You!
To: Sebastian Martinez
Subject: Hi there!

Hi Sebastian,
I've been in product development for 5 years now and I'd like to learn more about other marketing groups. I know you recently made the leap to data and analytics. Can we grab a cup of coffee one day so you can share the path you took? Thank you!
You

QUESTIONS TO HELP YOU GET STARTED

- Who can you ask for some time to chat, followed by a request for an introduction to someone new? Who could be the first domino in a series of meeting new people?

- Do you have a mentor or supervisor who could start your snowball of meeting new people?

- Are there particular departments that spark your interest? If so, should you tailor your request to lead you in that direction? For example, if you're interested in mergers and acquisitions, you might ask people you know if they have contacts in that department for an introduction.

- If you see someone you have a relationship with having a conversation with another person you'd also like to get to know, can you later ask for an introduction? Is there a mutual connection on social media?

- If you don't feel comfortable asking for a referral in a live conversation, could you do it afterward in a written thank-you note?

- Is there someone you mentor who you should ask if they need help in this area? You could say, "Is there a particular area of the company that interests you? If so, I may have a connection for you to explore."

TIP 6

Send Holiday Greetings

I love holidays, especially the end-of-year celebrations of Christmas, Hanukkah, Kwanzaa, and New Year's. I adore the sounds, scents, music, and joyfulness in the air. It seems as though there's an extra sense of comradery at work, whether it's holiday lunches, ugly sweater contests, cheerful decorations, or gift exchanges. And this is the time of year, more than any other, when I see glimpses of my colleagues' families and pets in their annual holiday cards. This makes them more human and real to me, and naturally leads to a richer understanding of diversity. I just love it.

I used to send a large stack of holiday cards via paper mail to many coworkers, both present and past, as a way to keep in touch. In recent years, I switched to scanning one in and emailing it out individually. Because I feel strongly about not sending mass blind-copied emails—more on that in tip 11—I send them individually with a dash of personalization.

I switched to a digital version for several reasons.

First, I try to consider the environmental impact. I love receiving holiday cards in the mail at home from family and friends, and I proudly display them in my kitchen. The colorful sight makes me smile, and I marvel at how my friends' kids have grown and how happy everyone looks in the photos. Yes, I'm fully aware these pictures don't even remotely represent reality. I realize that behind every smiling photo of a kid is a parent threatening to take away video games if they don't flash their pearly whites on command. But how do I handle it when I receive a card at work? If I'm honest, I enjoy opening it at the moment, but it doesn't get displayed. I look at the card with appreciation, and then it goes to a stack on my desk, which eventually moves to the declutter pile, which ultimately transfers to the recycling box. If I'm tossing the cards, I'm sure others are as well. At some point, it dawned on me that a digital version could be just as effective without cutting down as many trees.

Second, these cards are expensive! I've already mentioned I'm frugal. I've always been mercilessly teased by friends and family about my spending habits—I contend I'm *frugal*, not cheap; there's a difference—and I try to be intentional about spending money. Cards can be costly, and the fancier they are, the higher they're priced. I order over a hundred paper cards to send to friends and family because I know many of them display cards in their houses, just as I do. But for my colleagues at work, I now send an email.

Finally, an email lends itself to two-way communication. When I receive a paper card in the mail, I don't necessarily turn to my computer to type a note letting the sender know I received it. With an email, I can swiftly say thank you, comment about holiday plans, and compliment them on their happy-looking family—even if their kids did lose video games in the process.

The winter holidays are a perfect opportunity to send a greeting. Because I celebrate Hanukkah, and many of my colleagues celebrate Christmas, I choose to send a "Happy Holidays" greeting. I personally don't get offended if someone sends me Christmas wishes, as I'm grateful for the thought in any religious denomination. But some people may be sensitive to receiving a holiday greeting different than their own; hence an all-encompassing "Happy Holidays" is what I elect to send.

The following holiday greeting email was sent a few years ago and included a photo of my family. I know it's an old photo because now both children are taller than me, and one has blue hair!

From: Rachel Simon
To: Jennifer Diego
Subject: Happy Holidays!

Jennifer,
Happy holidays to you and your family! It is a pleasure working with you and I'm excited to see what you will do with the Women of Finance this year when you become President!

Best wishes for a terrific new year!

Rachel

From: Jennifer Diego
To: Rachel Simon
Subject: RE: Happy Holidays!

Thank you so much for the note and the beautiful picture of your family! Happy holidays to you and your family as well! I am excited about my role with Women of Finance next year and already have a few new ideas that I am working on with the Chairs. I'll look for a date in January when we can catch up over lunch to discuss further.

I hope you and your family take some time off at the end of the year to relax. Are you going away for vacation?

Jennifer

Jennifer's response was great and displayed the two-way communi-

Jennifer's response was great and displayed the two-way communication I referenced. She thanked me; complimented my family, which
always scores points; and ended with a question about vacation plans,
which I answered in a subsequent email. More importantly, I was
touched that she shared her excitement of being the incoming president of Women of Finance and that she wanted to hear my opinion on
her direction. Would she have set up a time for us to connect in January
regardless? Perhaps, but the email certainly lent itself to the request. I
imagine Jennifer felt terrific to receive my holiday greeting, and it made
me feel valued to receive the response that she wanted to discuss her
ideas with me.

You'll notice that the title of this chapter is "Send Holiday Greetings."
The title isn't "Send *Winter* Holiday Greetings." There are so many holidays throughout the year when you could apply this tip.

For instance, look at this email I received from a team member, Sherry,
on Boss's Day:

From: Sherry Penton
To: Rachel Simon
Subject: Happy Boss's Day!

Good morning Rachel!

As today is Boss's Day, I wanted to take a moment to thank you for all you do
for this organization and all you have done for me personally. I have learned
so much from you through your presentations and all the opportunities you
have given me to grow and develop. The opportunities stretch me and take
me out of what is comfortable and I love it! I wanted you to know how much
I appreciate the opportunities and how much I appreciate you.

Have a Happy Boss's Day!

Sherry

Wow! I was her boss's boss's boss. The email doesn't feel like networking, yet it is. It was warm, genuine, and intended to make my day, which it absolutely did. I felt validated that my efforts to lead were noticed, as I tried my best to engage employees at all levels. I had never thought of sending this type of greeting to my superiors at work, and it's such a lovely idea. By the way, Boss's Day is typically celebrated in October, if you want to mark your calendar. You can tuck this idea away for Administrative Professionals Day as well, which is typically celebrated in April.

I've learned to send emails for holidays I know are significant *to a particular person*. Lunar New Year's greetings for my Chinese colleagues and Ramadan Kareem greetings for my Muslim colleagues are two examples that are especially appreciated, as these holidays often go unnoticed in the workplace. I'm grateful when colleagues of other faiths send me Rosh Hashanah greetings for the Jewish New Year, even though they don't celebrate the same holiday. It shows cultural awareness and an open mind to diversity, which only enhances our working relationships. Here's an email I sent to Mohammed during Ramadan:

From: Rachel Simon
To: Mohammed Salem
Subject: Ramadan Kareem

Hi Mohammed,
Ramadan Kareem to you and your family! I like how you've taught me about your holiday. Does your family have a special tradition to break the daily fast?

You are such a wonderful colleague – generous, kind, and easy to be around. I truly enjoy working with you. Best wishes for a meaningful holiday.

Rachel

I've been taught a lot about other faiths just by asking for an education within these greetings, and I've developed profound relationships with colleagues by utilizing this simple tip. The greetings cost me nothing to send, but they often make a lasting, positive impression. The internet is a great source of information about the proper way to express holiday greetings, especially if it's a different culture than your own. I'd also encourage you not to overthink it. If you're worried about saying the wrong thing, you can skip the official greeting all together and simply say "I'm thinking of you during this special time." I know those thoughtful words would truly touch my heart.

I should add that I don't send an email for every holiday, as that would get old really fast, become predictable, and lose its intent. One colleague sends me a holiday greeting practically every month with a Valentine's or Saint Patrick's Day e-card. I appreciate that she takes the time to reach out, but it loses its luster with such frequency, especially for holidays that aren't important to me. It would be more meaningful if she reduced the rate and sent a thoughtful catch-up note instead.

What about other holidays and momentous events? I like to be recognized on my birthday, so I do my best to send emails to colleagues for theirs. If it's a co-worker I see often, I may send a quick note, or even a text, a fun meme, a GIF, etc. to express my birthday wishes. It's always nice to be thought of and remembered. I mean, who wouldn't want birthday wishes, especially since aging is a privilege denied to many? But if it's someone with whom I want to broaden a relationship, or with whom I want to reconnect because it's been a while, I don't merely say, "Happy Birthday," but instead I offer a deeper sentiment and/or a compliment. Additionally, I typically ask a simple question intended to promote a two-way dialogue, as illustrated in the example below.

From: Rachel Simon
To: Kate Brown
Subject: Happy Birthday!

Kate, it's your birthday – yay! I just wanted to tell you how much I appreciate your partnership and your friendship! It's such a pleasure working with you. Not only are you so good at what you do (and you get things done!), but you're also an amazing mom to your sweet babies and someone I admire.

Have a wonderful day and year ahead! Do you have plans to celebrate with your family?

Rachel

From: Kate Brown
To: Rachel Simon
Subject: RE: Happy Birthday!

Wow, Rachel, this is the best birthday note! It's great to have you compliment me on my work, but when you compliment me on my mothering skills, well, that is just the best. ☺ I've learned a lot from you and how you balance it all. I greatly admire you as well!!!

We're having a small get together this weekend with my parents. They can bring whatever flavor of cake they want as long as it's chocolate. LOL, I know we have that in common too! ☺ ☺ ☺

Thanks for the birthday note and for making my day!

Kate

I'm glad I took the time to send Kate such a personal birthday greeting, as her reaction suggested that the note meant a lot. I imagine it was a "keeper" of an email rather than just one to read and delete—for both of us. The fact that we share a passion for chocolate makes her a keeper in my networking circle. How would you feel receiving such a warm and personal greeting? *Remember: when done properly, networking makes people feel really good.*

To remember important dates, you may want to record colleagues' birthdays on your calendar as a recurring event. That way, even if you don't work together in proximity in the future, you'll still have the annual date pop up to remind you to reach out. Alternatively, if you employ an administrative assistant, you can ask for help keeping track of these special days.

I also send emails to colleagues for milestone career anniversaries, like the one below:

From: Rachel Simon
To: Selma Brizio
Subject: Your Service Anniversary!

Selma,

Congrats on 25 years of service – woo-hoo! I'm sure you've had many exciting roles over the years – what's been your favorite? Your most memorable?

I truly appreciate all that you do for our organization and for our company. Thank you for your dedication and for making this a great place to work!

Rachel

While it's extremely common at my company for someone to celebrate ten years of service, I similarly watch for opportunities, especially with new employees, to congratulate them on shorter milestones. It can be a big deal to reach even one year of employment and could mean the world to a colleague that someone noticed and remembered.

A great opportunity also exists to extend congratulations for significant events in colleagues' lives, such as births of children or grandchildren, weddings, etc. I was extremely touched to receive this email from my peer Thomas acknowledging my son's Bar Mitzvah.

From: Thomas Pulling
To: Rachel Simon
Subject: Mazel tov!

Rachel, I understand your son's Bar Mitzvah is this weekend. Mazel Tov! I know what a tremendous milestone this is for your family and I offer my heartfelt congratulations.

Enjoy this special time and I'd love to hear more (and see photos) next time we connect.

Thomas

This was such a beautiful, unexpected sentiment, and I felt special receiving these well-wishes. As a result, I now go out of my way to offer heartfelt congratulations for similar events, such as baptisms, confirmations, etc. I would not have thought to do that if someone hadn't modeled it for me. I love trickle-down networking inspiration!

Humans want to feel recognized and seen, especially during momentous events that are important to them. Sending an email or digital card literally costs nothing aside from time and energy, yet it may go a long way to developing a deep relationship.

READY TO TRY?

Here are some sample emails to get your creative juices flowing. Edit them to fit your own writing style and unique situation.

From: You!
To: Wang Li Chang
Subject: Happy New Year!

Wang Li,

I know it's the Lunar New Year and want to extend warm wishes to you and your family!

Do you have special traditions? Special foods that you prepare? I'd love to learn more!

From: You!
To: John Forrest
Subject: Veteran's Day

John,

If I remember correctly, you served in the Air Force. I just want to say thank you for your service and know that you are thought of and appreciated.

How many years were you in the service and where were you stationed?

From: You!
To: Shoshana Cohen
Subject: Happy Passover

Shoshana,
I want to wish you a very happy Passover. I know this is an important holiday for you and your family – are you hosting a Seder this year at your home?

Best wishes for a meaningful holiday with your loved ones.

From: You!
To: Amit Khatri
Subject: Happy Diwali!

Hi Amit,
May the illuminating lights surround you and your loved ones with happiness and positivity. You create such a positive light in our office and I wish you much prosperity and health in the year ahead. What are your family traditions?

Happy Diwali!

From: You!
To: Bree Smith
Subject: Happy Easter

Hi Bree,
Happy Easter to you and your loved ones! I know this one will be particularly special as you spend the holiday with all of your grandchildren! I hope you have a meaningful time at church and then afterward with your egg hunt.

I would love to see photos of the little ones coloring their eggs! Enjoy the weekend.

From: You!
To: Gloria Escobar
Subject: Happy birthday!

Gloria,
I am thinking of you today and wishing you a wonderful birthday! You're a terrific colleague who constantly makes me laugh and de-stress. Your smile lights up the room and you're an absolute joy to be around!

I appreciate your partnership and most importantly, your friendship! What are your plans to celebrate this weekend?

From: You!
To: Jonathon Wexler
Subject: Happy work anniversary!

Hi Jonathon,
Congratulations on your one-year work anniversary! You've been such an amazing member of our team, it's hard to believe it's only been a year that you've been here. I've enjoyed being your supervisor, and now your peer, since your recent promotion. I'm super proud of you!

What have you enjoyed the most about working here?

QUESTIONS TO HELP YOU GET STARTED

- Who should you send a December holiday greeting to? Do you want to include a photo of your family for a personal connection?
- How can you make the email visually appealing? An image brightens up any holiday greeting. You can search for free holiday clip art images on any search website, as they are abundant and plentiful.
- Who is celebrating a holiday that is different from your own? Should you send an email asking about customs, traditions, food, and memories? If you're uncertain of a holiday's significance, consider doing a quick internet search on the best way to express a greeting.
- Who do you work with that has an upcoming birthday or milestone anniversary?

- How will you compile a list of birthdays and service anniversaries? Can human resources provide it, or should you simply ask your coworkers for the dates?
- Are there other significant events to recognize, such as weddings, births, religious milestones, etc.?

TIP 7

Have Structure to the Networking Session

I remember the first day of my career as if it occurred yesterday. I moved solo from Austin to Kansas City, and after much anticipation and apprehension, the day finally arrived for me to report to my new workplace. I woke up early and paid extra attention to my carefully selected first-day-of-work outfit and personal appearance because I wanted to make a great first impression. I departed with plenty of time to navigate the new roads and arrived at the building earlier than expected. Instead of entering the office early, which in hindsight may have shown initiative and enthusiasm, I drove my car around the building three times before I could convince myself to park. I was *that* nervous and thought I would pass out from anxiety. I eventually did put one foot in front of the other to walk in, only to realize I was wearing one black shoe and one blue shoe. Gah! It was too late, and there was no time to go home and change, since I had whittled away my extra time working up the nerve to walk into the building. It's a good thing no one noticed. Just kidding. Everyone noticed, but they were too kind to make fun of me on my first day. That came later once we got to know each other.

Have you ever been so nervous that you did something similar? The answer is likely yes, as we all have our "black-shoe, blue-shoe moments." A colleague was once so edgy before a presentation that she left her reading glasses at home, which would have been fine had her material been memorized, but alas, she needed to read note cards. Another colleague was so anxious about a meeting that he mixed up the unlabeled flash drive with his presentation among other flash drives and had to sort through them all—in the front of the room while everyone stared at him in silence. Our embarrassing "black-shoe, blue-shoe" moments eventually become comical stories, but they're sorely painful to live through at the time.

Surprisingly, I don't recall ever being so nervous before a networking session that I forgot my own name or other basic information about myself. I say surprisingly because it seems like something that this shy, introverted woman might easily have done. Have I been nervous before big meetings and presentations? Absolutely. Actually, every single time, even to this day. But I can't say I've ever been over-the-top-apprehensive before a one-on-one coffee meeting or networking lunch, since I'm so much more relaxed in small group settings. Several of my colleagues, however, have indeed confessed to struggling with this. One peer told me that she once felt extremely prepared for a networking meeting, but when the time came she was so anxious she couldn't remember a single interesting fact about herself, let alone any profound questions to ask. She knew the networking session fell embarrassingly flat and wasn't astonished that it ended up as a one-time-only event with no follow-up session. She asked me how she could avoid this in the future.

Fortunately, there's a simple solution: have structure to the networking session.

I met with Whitney for a coffee meeting, and after we sat down with our beverages she pulled out this one-page document to guide the conversation:

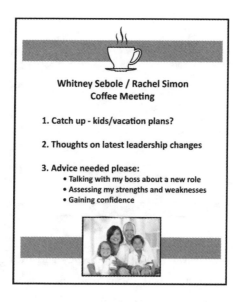

Whitney Sebole / Rachel Simon
Coffee Meeting

1. Catch up - kids/vacation plans?

2. Thoughts on latest leadership changes

3. Advice needed please:
   - Talking with my boss about a new role
   - Assessing my strengths and weaknesses
   - Gaining confidence

I love that she came prepared with an agenda to put herself at ease. With a quick scan, it gave me insight into what she was hoping to gain from the session. Including the photo of her family was an ingenious addition, as we began the conversation with a discussion about our children and then smoothly moved through the rest of her outline. It's also a great example of understanding your audience. Most people know I'd love to see photos of their families, while others might find this a little out of place. Try to gauge who you're meeting with to understand if you should keep the agenda strictly professional or add a mix of personal information as well.

I met Matt at a training class several years ago. He lived in New York and asked for some time on my calendar for a virtual coffee. Before our phone conversation, he sent me this slide about himself via email:

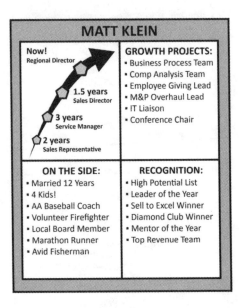

How clever! The top box showed the jobs he's held, the right box exhibited growth projects, and the bottom quadrants displayed recognition he's earned and activities he enjoys on the side, like running, fishing, and serving as a volunteer firefighter. It was impressive to see it laid out in this type of dashboard, and it aided our conversation. He didn't need to send a full résumé, since this was a networking session, not an interview, yet I gained a lot of the same information in a more creative manner.

Whether or not you bring a printed agenda, you should carefully consider what you'll talk about when you meet, regardless of if it's the first or the twentieth time. If you're the one who asked for the meeting, this is imperative. Don't put the burden on the invitee to lead the conversation. You *must* come prepared to engage in a dialogue—I cannot stress this enough!

When I invite someone to a networking session, the question I start with is, "Would you mind telling me about yourself and your career journey?" Most people love to talk about themselves; therefore it's an easy way to break the ice and gain quick engagement. It's less risky than beginning with personal questions that may be off-putting if I don't know the person's style yet.

I'm also prepared to answer the same question about my own career journey in a concise manner if I'm asked, "How about you?" I quickly lose interest when people tell me year by year about their jobs. Yawn! It's important to be able to offer a brief high-level overview. Here's something similar to what I say:

> I've been with the company since college and spent many years working my way up through call centers as a manager, area manager, and director. When I was promoted to an assistant vice president, it was in credit and collections, which was a great pivot for me. In this job, I once again led call centers, which I knew well, but it was on the finance side of the business, which really stretched me. In time, I was tapped to be a vice president in finance and then in customer care. Recently, my career took a complete left-hand turn when I was asked to be a vice president in privacy, which is where I am now. This is an emerging space—it has been invigorating and energizing to be a part of this organization, where I lead a team of about fifty privacy professionals.

I don't recite these words verbatim, but it's similar to how I describe my career at a high level each time. Guess how long that takes? Less than forty-five seconds. I timed it. Too often, I meet with people who endlessly drone on about every single job they've ever had. We don't even get to other questions, because they ramble too long about the very first one. I've practiced delivering a crisp way to articulate my background, and then I watch for cues to talk more in depth about a particular experience if the other person shows interest.

The next question I typically ask is, "What are you working on right now?" or "What are your challenges?" Notice this is a different question than asking, "What's new?" or "How's your job?" as it's more specific and will lead to a meaningful answer. Here's the key to this tip: As I listen to the answer, I ask myself, "What do I know that might be helpful to this person?" For instance, if she tells me she's working on employee engagement issues, I might respond, "Let me tell you what my organization is doing to improve employee engagement." If the person shares that he has an attendance issue with his team members, I might reply, "I don't have that particular issue right now. But several years ago, I faced attendance issues all the time, and here's how I approached it."

Listening is such an essential skill, but having a dialogue—with a give and a take, an ebb and a flow—is even more vital. The relationships I enjoy the most, and the ones that have evolved from networking to mentoring relationships, are the ones in which I equally offer and receive knowledge, experience, and advice. It's lovely when I'm asked my opinion, and, of course, it makes me feel important when people hang on to every word— if only it were always that way with my children! Yet I genuinely enjoy learning from other people as well. I want to be inspirational, but I also want to be inspired. I want to impart nuggets of wisdom, but I also want to learn others' points of view. Sometimes, if the other person is too shy to offer her opinion, I may ask, "How would you respond to that question?" But don't necessarily wait for your viewpoint to be asked—learn to engage in a dialogue.

Where does the conversation go from there? It depends on who I'm meeting with and what I hope to gain from the meeting. If I'm seeking education about someone's job, my questions may be focused on their responsibilities and skills. If I'm looking for guidance, my questions may be focused on key learnings and advice. If I'm hoping to establish or improve a relationship through comradery, my questions may be focused on projects we're working on together and personal questions about hobbies and family.

I'm always prepared with at least ten questions in the back of my mind to ask. These are questions that can't be answered with a simple yes or no and might include:

1. What's a typical day like for you?
2. Why did you decide to pursue the career you did?
3. What skills are required in your organization?
4. If you could start all over again, what would you change about your path?
5. What is the best part of your job?
6. What are some mistakes you've learned from along the way?
7. Is there a good book or video you'd recommend on leadership?
8. What do you think are the top skills needed in the workplace of the future?
9. What types of people do you enjoy working with the most?
10. What makes people stand out to you? How do superstars catch your attention?

Clearly, this isn't an exhaustive list, but it's designed to get your wheels turning. You want to appear relaxed and confident, no matter how nervous you are, and you don't want the person to feel under attack with rapid-fire questions as if it were an interview. It may be helpful to practice with a trusted peer asking questions in a comfortable manner that lends itself to a two-way conversation and a fulfilling dialogue.

If I'm meeting someone for lunch in person, I should note that my walking-to-the-restaurant conversation is very lighthearted. For instance, I may ask, "What did you do this weekend?" or "Do you have plans to get outside to enjoy this beautiful weather?" while we walk rather than ask a more profound question like the ones I listed above. If we meet for coffee and need to order first, I'll keep the conversation to breezy chitchat while we stand in line and save my meatier questions for when we sit down with drinks in hand. Similarly, if the networking session is in the office or via video, I ease into the conversation with questions such as, "How is your week going?" before I engage in the deeper questions that are on my mind.

I want to stress one concept again because it's important enough to repeat: If you're the one setting up the networking session, it's up to *you* to come prepared to engage in conversation. Sure, the other person might take the lead, especially if she's a level or two higher than you, but you need to be prepared to guide the conversation with questions. Don't leave any unused time on the table, as it's critical to have enough questions in your back pocket to last the entire time. Don't wrap up early because you have nothing to say. I once met with a new employee who asked for some time with me, which I was more than happy to provide. But the meeting quickly turned dull when she had no questions to ask me, and she answered the conversation-starter questions I had of her with one-word answers. It was excruciating, and time crawled by at a snail's pace. After a long ten minutes, we ended the meeting, and I never heard from her again. It was painful—I'm sure for her as well as me—and an excellent reminder to be both interested *and* interesting.

I conclude the networking session with a warm farewell by telling the other person just how much I appreciated our discussion and cite a few key takeaways. If the meeting went well—and I know immediately in my gut if it did—I ask if we could meet again, and then I take responsibility for setting up our next session later in the year. I pay a genuine compliment about a wise viewpoint, a sunny outlook on life, an impeccable reputation, or another character trait that resonated with me. *Remember: when done properly, networking makes people feel really good.* What would cause this person to want to meet with me again to develop a relationship? Here are a few examples of what I may say as I wrap up the conversation:

- "I've truly enjoyed our time together and loved your insights on work-life balance. I'm inspired to discuss recommendations that could work well in my situation with my supervisor. Thanks for sharing your story, which gives me courage! I will keep in touch and let you know how it goes."
- "I had been looking forward to our time together, and you didn't disappoint! I got more out of it than I had even hoped. Thanks for sharing your knowledge about your department and what skills you think are important for the future, as I trust your judgment. I'd like to keep in touch. Mind if I schedule some time again in a quarter or so?"
- "Thank you so much for meeting with me today. I can see why people think so highly of you. You were very generous with your time, and I know how busy you are. I plan to order the book you suggested, and I'm sure I'll take away some good nuggets based on your recommendation. Is it OK if I schedule time on your calendar again midyear to continue our discussion?"

If I'm the one who requested the meeting, I'll also write a thank-you note, with specific references to what we discussed—more on that in tip 12.

How long should networking sessions last? Well, it depends on a lot of factors, especially the cultural norms of your company. For instance, my lunches are usually sixty minutes, which includes meeting in the lobby and walking to and from a nearby restaurant. Some of you may only have time for thirty minutes—if you typically eat at your desk while you work, thirty minutes may even seem luxurious—while others may take two hours (nice!). My coffee meetings are always thirty minutes, for both virtual and in person. For some of you, fifteen minutes might be perfect, especially if it's a new introduction to someone who always appears to be busy. When I meet with someone higher than me, I typically block the subsequent thirty minutes on my calendar in case the session starts or ends late or, even better, if it runs overtime because we have so much to discuss. It's always awesome when that happens! I would feel awkward and anxious if I had to tell someone in a higher position that I need to cut our time short to get to another meeting; therefore I ensure I don't have somewhere critical to be directly after our session. Despite my best efforts to avoid this predicament, I occasionally need to be the one to end the meeting due to a time crunch. When this happens, I tactfully say, "I want to be respectful of your time, and I know we have run over, so I will close by saying thank you. I'm very grateful for your time." Alternatively, I believe it's acceptable to state I need to work on a deliverable for my boss or a customer. In this case, I might say, "I've enjoyed this so much, but I do need to head back to my desk to take care of a pressing issue."

To close this chapter, I'm going to reiterate a critical point one more time: If you're requesting the networking session, *you* must be the one to come prepared to lead the conversation. You want the other person to feel like he just made the best use of his own precious time, so plan accordingly!

READY TO TRY?

Unlike previous chapters, I don't have sample emails to show you, as this tip is designed for a live conversation.

Below are ten additional questions you may want to ask:

1. What have been the keys to your success?
2. How do you balance work and home life?

3. Where do you get sources of information about our industry?

4. What do you look for in a successful employee?

5. How do you manage upward with your boss?

6. What has been a challenging time in your career, and how did you overcome it?

7. What do you think about the various ways our industry has been in the news?

8. How do you manage internal politics and culture?

9. Early in your career, how did you gain exposure?

10. Who do you consider to be your mentor, and how have you nurtured that relationship?

Here's an additional format for a one-page document to guide your discussion.

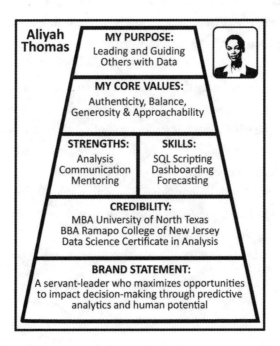

QUESTIONS TO HELP YOU GET STARTED

- What are you hoping to get out of the networking session, such as comradery, advice, knowledge, or mentorship?
- How should you structure the dialogue for your desired result? What are ten questions you can have in the back of your mind to keep the conversation flowing?
- Are you more comfortable having conversations while sitting face-to-face or walking side by side? While having lunch or drinking coffee? What's the optimal environment to help facilitate your goals for the discussion?
- Would a one-page document help you feel more comfortable to guide the conversation? How would you design it to make it visually appealing with photos or agenda items?
- What level of preparation do you need to be able to ask informed questions? Are you equipped to answer the same questions if you're asked your viewpoint in return?
- How long should you schedule the session for? How will you keep track of time during the conversation to ensure you don't run over?
- Is there any public information available about the person you're meeting with, such as a recent promotion announcement, a blog article, a LinkedIn profile, or an online interview? This may help guide the conversation with relevant questions.
- What are the best networking sessions you've ever attended, and why? What did you appreciate about the flow and dialogue that you can emulate in future meetings?

TIP 8

Invest in Relationships When Work Is Tough

I wish I could say all my work assignments go smoothly, but they don't. I wish I could say I never have problems with my tasks, but I do. I wish I could say I get along perfectly with everyone, but I don't. You may find that last one hard to believe, with my dazzling personality and all, but sadly it's true. What I've noticed about human nature is that when relationships are contentious, and when things aren't going so well, it's our tendency to pull back defensively and respond along the lines of, "If she isn't going to be nice, I'm not going to be nice. If he's going to hoard info, I'll hoard info. If she's going to make this difficult, then so will I." Kind of like five-year-olds, except worse, because we know better. Have you been there? I certainly have. I'm a positive, optimistic person, and as I shared in tip 5, one of the secrets of my success is that I'm easy to work with; therefore I loathe negative, petty behavior and immediately stop it if I find it's my own. I don't enjoy working with challenging people. How could they possibly enjoy working with me if I act in the same manner?

Over the years, I've discovered that one of the most important times to form relationships and to develop allies is when things aren't going smoothly. I refer to such rough conditions as being "in the trenches." From military origins, this phrase often refers to a long, arduous, unrewarding task with the strong possibility of significant pain being inflicted. That sounds like an accurate description of some of the daunting jobs I've experienced! I use the phrase when results are tough on a project, when things aren't moving fast enough, and when it feels like I'm under attack from all sides. I want to hunker down and just try not to get hit. Ah, fun times. Perhaps it sounds familiar.

To take the military analogy even further, I must reference a speech by Admiral William McRaven. I had the chance—scratch that: I had the *honor and privilege*—to hear Admiral McRaven speak, during which he discussed several insights he learned throughout his impressive career with the US Navy and as a commander with Special Operations. If you want to be inspired, I encourage you to listen to his 2014 commencement speech at the University of Texas. In the speech, he discussed a concept from Navy SEAL basic training about being a "sugar cookie":

> Several times a week, the instructors would line up the class and do a uniform inspection. It was exceptionally thorough. Your hat had to be perfectly starched, your uniform immaculately pressed, and your belt buckle shiny and void of any smudges. But it seemed that no matter how much effort you put into starching your hat or pressing your uniform or polishing your belt buckle, it just wasn't good enough. The instructors would find "something" wrong.
>
> For failing the uniform inspection, the student had to run, fully clothed into the surf zone and then, wet from head to toe, roll around on the beach until every part of your body was covered with sand. The effect was known as a "sugar cookie." You stayed in that uniform the rest of the day—cold, wet, and sandy.

> There were many a student who just couldn't accept the fact that all their effort was in vain. That no matter how hard they tried to get the uniform right, it was unappreciated. Those students didn't make it through training. Those students didn't understand the purpose of the drill. You were never going to succeed. You were never going to have a perfect uniform.
>
> **Sometimes, no matter how well you prepare or how well you perform, you still end up as a sugar cookie. It's just the way life is sometimes.**

I listened to that part of his speech multiple times, and I frequently use his phrase in the workplace. How many times have I meticulously prepared for a meeting, even had positive, encouraging news to deliver, and I *still* got pummeled? It's so unfair, and I think to myself, *I was just sugar-cookied*! The best way to minimize sugar-cookie potential is to have allies. And the only way to ensure having strong allies is to intentionally develop and maintain relationships.

The following email is an excellent example of a colleague being supportive during a difficult situation. I accepted a new position in June, and when I did I inherited a project in which we were on year three of a one-year plan to integrate several systems. Needless to say, it was going fantastic, if your interpretation of fantastic is excruciating pain. During biweekly conference calls with many senior managers, there was a lot of finger-pointing and blame assigned. What's the opposite of gentle and fun? That's how I'd describe those meetings. On one of the calls, my colleague Jack paid me a compliment. I was very appreciative—and astonished—and when the call was complete, we had the following email exchange:

From: Rachel Simon
To: Jack Dakota
Subject: Appreciation

Hi Jack,
Your compliment to me on today's call means more than you know. Thanks for being such a great partner.
Rachel

From: Jack Dakota
To: Rachel Simon
Subject: RE: Appreciation

Rachel,
You are delightful to work with. You are straightforward, willing to take on tough issues, and VERY collaborative.
Jack

What? I had no idea. I literally had no idea that's what he thought of me. Leading up to this point, I was feeling very insecure, wondering if any of my efforts would yield results, since I wasn't gaining any traction. I was suffering a massive lack of confidence, as this was my first vice-president role, and I was struggling to accomplish anything in a productive manner. This exchange literally changed the whole trajectory of the project. I assumed my role in June, this note was written in October, and we had the issue solved by January. It gave me the shot of confidence I desperately needed. After this, we arranged an in-person meeting with our teams to outline a solution and design a new approach to the problems that had plagued us. The in-person meeting was exactly what was required, and we actually had a good time approaching the problem with a renewed sense of empowerment and unity.

It was such an important lesson for me. We need colleagues who will pay us compliments in front of others when things are hard. We need coworkers to champion our progress and ideas. It's great to have strong relationships with colleagues when things are going well, but they're even more important when we find ourselves navigating rough waters. And let's face it, many of our jobs are tough and we find ourselves in rough waters more often than we'd like. It's not enough that we don't want to drown—we want to swim and thrive and enjoy our work.

I've learned even when things are challenging not to pull back and retreat toward ineffective behavior. That has never gotten me anywhere. It's actually more accurate to say that it's gotten me *somewhere*, but nowhere good, helpful, or productive. Instead, I've learned to use this as a tool to lift someone's spirits. If I'm feeling down and beaten up, chances are the other person is too. *Remember: when done properly, networking makes people feel really good.*

I regularly have one-on-one meetings with my supervisor and with my direct reports, but I also schedule regular individual sessions with key colleagues in other organizations. Partnerships and collaboration are critical for success in every role I've had throughout my career and regular touchpoints serve to keep our relationships solid and on track. For instance, in my role in finance, I required a close relationship with my peer in another department. The relationship started out somewhat contentious, as I was sometimes surprised by info he presented at meetings to senior leaders. The info was always accurate but presented in ways that advanced a different agenda from mine and didn't showcase my team's work in the best light. Needless to say, I was often frustrated as I exited meetings and I found myself feeling very discouraged and beat up. I was in the trenches, deep in the trenches. I knew I needed him as an ally, so I sent him this note to improve our relationship:

From: Rachel Simon
To: Jay Carlisle
Subject: One-on-one meetings?

Hi Jay, I hope all is well with you.

We have our work cut out for us to achieve our targets this year! I think it would be good for us to be on the same page before we have our senior-management readouts so we can make sure we're aligned on strategies.

Are you OK if I schedule some regular time for us to chat and catch up on issues? I am thinking 30 minutes every other week. Sound OK? I truly appreciate the partnership!

Rachel

From: Jay Carlisle
To: Rachel Simon
Subject: RE: One-on-one meetings?

More than OK, Rachel. Great idea. Looking forward to connecting on a regular basis.

Jay

During our first meeting, I discovered Jay felt similarly to how I did. He needed me as a strong and reliable partner, just as I needed him. It took just one note to break the ice to develop the relationship. We agreed to meet every other week and established a warm and productive relationship. In the first few minutes, we would catch up on personal chitchat, such as our families, vacations, etc. The rest of the time we would spend on business issues as we aligned our priorities and shared, as opposed to hoarded, information. We became true partners who worked together to meet a common goal, and there were plenty of opportunities for both of our teams to shine.

What do you do if a relationship is exceptionally strained? What if the existence of some baggage makes it difficult to move on with a collaborative spirit? To be honest, I've never personally been in this situation, but I've mentored several colleagues who have. The advice I've given is to have a sincere conversation with the person in which they accept full accountability, which opens the door to resolution. I've helped several mentees craft a message like the one below:

From: Rachel's Mentee
To: Stephanie Lee
Subject: Time to talk?

Hi Stephanie,
I've been doing some reflection, and I think I may have mishandled our relationship in the past. I'd love the chance to talk things over, to apologize for anything I may have done or said to jeopardize our partnership, and have a fresh start. Not only do I admire you, but I appreciate the type of leader that you are.

Are you open to grabbing a cup of coffee? If so, I will get that scheduled.

Thanks for the consideration.

Rachel's Mentee

The mentees who have taken this approach have reported enormous success. They were terrified to send the email but felt a wave of relief when it was received in such a positive manner. One mentee used this approach with her supervisor and got their relationship back on a smooth track filled with mutual respect. I was very proud of her, as I can think of few stressors in life worse than having a strained relationship with a boss or colleague and coming to work every day with a knot in your stomach. The keys to the email and the subsequent conversations are to take accountability, not place blame, pay a compliment if appropriate, and approach the meeting with an open mind to determine a path forward.

For some colleagues, an email may be enough to get the relationship on the right path. For others, a face-to-face meeting or live conversation may be in order. Be sure to understand your audience and what's required. Do you need to apologize, even if you aren't 100 percent to blame? Do you need to extend an olive branch even though you may have been nothing but collaborative and helpful? Give careful consideration beforehand of what may be expected to advance the situation.

The most important point is to be willing to accept feedback and criticism without becoming defensive. My dad, who has undoubtedly been among my most trusted career counselors, once gave me sound advice. He said, "If your verbalization of an open-door policy is no more than an empty platitude, don't bother to say you have one. If you really mean it, and your door is truly open for feedback, you should welcome all communications. But you need to be prepared to listen, take it all in, and then act upon that feedback." That's sage advice. If you set up the meeting yet plan to react in a self-justifying manner, it's sure to end poorly. If you plan to listen and graciously accept comments or constructive criticism, the situation is ripe for turning things around. It may take time for things to improve. If it's a critical relationship, keep at it. Cup of coffee by cup of coffee, conversation by conversation, it will likely turn around, but it may take time and effort to build trust on both sides. At the very least, your efforts will show vulnerability and transparency. And always remember that actions speak louder than words.

Please note I'm *not* encouraging you to engage in toxic conversations that make you feel belittled, harassed, or forced to endure yelling and cursing. There are plenty of qualified authors to seek out if you find yourself in this type of negative environment and don't know how to handle it. Rather, this advice is aimed at those who have the self-awareness to realize they may have some work to do to get a relationship on track to be productive and collaborative.

I hope you'll give some strong consideration to this tip. It's definitely one of the harder ones to implement—to invest in a relationship that may be strained or damaged—but it's one of the most rewarding and can change the course of a project or relationship. At a minimum, it may help avoid being sugar-cookied, and that's absolutely worth the time investment!

READY TO TRY?

Here are some sample emails to get your creative juices flowing. Edit them to fit your own writing style and unique situation.

From: You!
To: Claudia Cook
Subject: Welcome back to the team!

Hello Claudia,
I just heard that you're re-joining our team after working with another department for a year. This is wonderful news – you bring such a wealth of information and your curious, optimistic personality is terrific to be around.

The last time we worked together was tense and we didn't part on the best of terms. Can we start over as you re-join the team? I have so much respect for you and all your contributions. I'd love to clear the air over a virtual cup of coffee. Thoughts?

From: You!
To: Noah Leopold
Subject: Happy Friday

Hello Noah,
It's been a rough week and things didn't go as smoothly as I had hoped with the financial update. Can we chat for a few minutes via video to discuss how to get things back on track?

Thank you – I appreciate and value your partnership!

From: You!
To: LaKesha Jones
Subject: Our meeting earlier...

LaKesha,
It was good to hear your voice on our conference call earlier today. Things are tough with this new product launch and I just wanted to say thank you for hanging in there with our team. Thank you for the guidance and feedback – we will recalibrate.

Progress is happening (slowly but surely) – thank you for your partnership. I appreciate your positive, yet direct approach. I want to make you proud.

From: You!
To: Felicia Donaldson
Subject: Getting on the same page

Felicia,
It's becoming clear that our team may have taken on more work than our resources and capabilities will allow. I'm sure we can work together to find a compromise as we make some tough decisions. Thank you for your patience as we work through this.

From: You!
To: Rico Garcia
Subject: I appreciate the kind words...

Hi Rico,
That was a challenging meeting earlier today. I appreciate you chiming in about how hard our team is working. It was the bright spot of a really tough day to have our work recognized. Thank you so much – it went a long way with the team.

I understand you're coming to town next week – do you have time for a cup of coffee?

From: You!
To: Claire Monten
Subject: Kudos for a successful presentation

Claire,
I thought our presentation to our boss today was the best we've had. He had no idea our teams have had a rough time working together and I'm glad we've been able to keep the disagreements behind the scenes. Everyone is passionate about the outcome and that is leading us to do great things. We are making progress.

Just want to say thank you and that I appreciate your candid feedback that led us to such a successful presentation. Until the next one!

QUESTIONS TO HELP YOU GET STARTED

- Who do you need as an ally? Think about your challenging projects that may be moving at a poor or slow pace.

- Who would you benefit from having on your side when things are not going well? Consider those colleagues who are higher than you or in a position of influence.
- Who should you reach out to for advice on an issue that is demanding?
- Who should you have a fresh-start conversation with that would improve your stress level and/or professional success?
- If you need to resolve a conflict, what aspects could you compromise on to advance the relationship?
- Who should you publicly thank for their support? Who should you pay a compliment to or deliver words of gratitude in front of others? How do you showcase others in a positive light, especially when things are tough?
- Do you currently have a challenging relationship with a coworker? Can you think about it overnight and commit to resolving it the next day so it doesn't fester?

TIP 9

Deepen Relationships with People You Work Around

work on a large, sprawling floor at my company. There is space for at least two hundred people on our floor alone, a bright, open space with multiple areas for collaboration. There are some employees from my own team and also from other departments. You've likely heard the term *casual acquaintances*, which refers to people we encounter in a somewhat vague, infrequent environment. They're not considered friends per se, but rather friendly contacts. Well, I've adopted the term *casual strangers*. I'm surrounded by them. When we pass each other, we have a glint of recognition in our eyes as though we know each other. But in reality, we don't. I'm welcoming and cheerful, and they're equally welcoming and cheerful. They smile when we pass and say, "How are you?" I smile and respond, "Good, and you?" But for the most part, we don't even know each other's names.

If I were to challenge myself to quickly make a list of three people I work with on my floor but don't know, it would be simple. My list of these coworkers would look like this:

1. The tall man with the infectious smile who says good morning to me *every time* he sees me. Although I pass by him often, I don't know his name or what he does.

2. The recent grad who I frequently see in the café refilling our coffee cups. We've even had full-blown conversations about the weather and weekend activities, yet I know neither her name nor her role with the company.

3. The boisterous, happy, joyful gentleman who brings a lot of energy to the floor. Everyone seems to like him, but I've never had a conversation with him. I don't know his full name or what he does.

Now let's take it a step further. If I were to challenge myself to make a list of three additional people I work *around* but don't know, it would be just as easy. It would look like this:

1. Meredith—We attend a weekly call together and we've never had a conversation. I think we'd have a lot in common based on comments I've heard her make.

2. Lee—He's in a separate organization but supports mine. I only hear his name in a favorable light, and my team mentions him often as someone who is a great partner.

3. Dev—I receive reports from him with some marketing results. Beyond receiving these emails, we've never interacted.

These lists were quickly assembled, literally off the top of my head. I could add dozens of other names within mere minutes. I share these real examples for two reasons: First, to illustrate that there are abundant opportunities to network with coworkers with whom we have some familiarity. We just need to take advantage of them. Second, to show you how I'm personally a continual work in progress. If you think I know everyone at my company due to my networking, I'm confessing that I don't even know the names of half the people on my very own floor. I, too, sit next to people and don't know anything about them other than what they contributed to the topic at hand.

What's stopping us from reaching out to deepen relationships with people we already have some familiarity with? What's preventing us from turning a casual stranger into a casual acquaintance—which, with some nurturing, could turn into a trusted colleague, friend, or mentor? Here's my list of reasons why I might not reach out:

- Fear of being rejected—I'm an introvert. It's scary to walk up to someone I don't know well. It's frightening to approach someone new, especially with the predetermined thought that they might look at me sideways. For me, there are few horrors like being rejected or humiliated, especially if others are around to witness.
- Intimidation—What if the person has a massive job? What if she is a level or two higher? What if she thinks I'm silly for reaching out to introduce myself?
- Time—I am swamped during the day. Like most people, I'm incredibly busy. Every minute I spend talking with someone could be a minute I need to spend working late to finish. I could easily sell myself the story that I don't have time to network.
- Self-confidence—I often suffer from a lack of courage and imposter syndrome. Am I bold enough to say hello and introduce myself? Will they talk negatively about me behind my back? Am I just being paranoid?

What would you add? Cultural barriers and social norms may be a roadblock for some of you. For instance, I personally have never had an issue inviting someone of a different gender to engage in a conversation. For some, however, this may be inconceivable. These days I don't hesitate to ask coworkers about their culture, background, or country of origin. But the fear of coming across as miseducated or offensive may hold you back; therefore you may find it's not worth the risk and determine it's more comfortable to say nothing.

Now let's look at the exact same examples with a new lens—the one that is based on the premise that *when done properly, networking makes people feel really good.*

- The tall man with the infectious smile—What if I were to say, "I appreciate it when you greet me with a smile and a good morning every day! I'm going to put my stuff down in my office and then grab a cup of coffee. Want to join me?" I expect he would feel terrific that I noticed him and extended an invitation.

- The recent grad—What if the next time I see her at the coffee machine I were to say, "We seem to keep bumping into each other, and I don't even know your name. Tell me a little about yourself while the coffee brews. Are you new to the company?" I imagine she would feel more engaged and welcomed.

- The boisterous, happy, joyful gentleman—What if tomorrow I were to tell him that I was thinking about who brightens my day with positive energy, and he immediately came to mind? I expect he would feel amazing that someone recognized him.

- Meredith, Lee, and Dev—What if I were to follow up with an email such as those in the "Ready to Try?" section to get to know them better? I anticipate we would find things we have in common, learn how our work overlaps, and discover ways to assist one another. At a minimum, I would brighten their days.

The following is an example of how I worked to deepen a relationship with someone I already knew. A few years ago, I closely coordinated with

Jansen to prepare one of our senior officers for a webcast we were both somewhat in charge of. We needed to collaborate since we each owned a piece. I had worked around Jansen for many years and thought very highly of him, but our paths had never really crossed until this project. Once it was over, we exchanged this note:

From: Rachel Simon
To: Jansen Martin
Subject: Today's Webcast

Hi Jansen, I thought that John did great on the webcast. It went really well – thank you for your help!

Rachel

From: Jansen Martin
To: Rachel Simon
Subject: RE: Today's Webcast

Yes, I was able to watch the webcast. Thought he did a great job. Nice working with you on this project.

Jansen

From: Rachel Simon
To: Jansen Martin
Subject: RE: Today's Webcast

Likewise! I am sure we will have the opportunity again!
Hey, let's grab lunch one day. While we have worked around each other for several years, it would be great to get to know you better.

Rachel

From: Jansen Martin
To: Rachel Simon
Subject: RE: Today's Webcast

Sounds great. I will get something on the calendar after next week. Trying to take time off before quarter ends. Looking forward to it!

Jansen

I like this email exchange for several reasons. First, it closed the loop on the project we worked hard on together. Sometimes we get so distracted with all that is on our plates that we fail to stop and show appreciation to the people who helped make it successful. Second, it demonstrates just how easy it is to continue a connection. I simply said, "Do you want to grab lunch one day?" I didn't do a whole big wind up and say, "If you aren't too busy ... if you don't think I'm out of line by asking . . ." I just informally asked to schedule lunch, he enthusiastically accepted, and that was the start of our deeper relationship.

Another example is my relationship with Chengcheng, who I met while serving on a diversity and inclusion council. After a few months of group meetings with about twenty other council members, I reached out individually to see if we could talk, just the two of us. I sent him the following email:

From: Rachel Simon
To: Chengcheng Yan
Subject: D&I Council

Hi Chengcheng,
I know you enjoy serving on the Diversity and Inclusion Council as much as I do. We are engaged in such fulfilling work! I appreciated the remarks you made today and your comments really made me think differently.

Mind if I schedule time for us to talk a bit more? I'd love to pick your brain about some topical issues. Thanks!
Rachel

Chengcheng and I had an enlightening and meaningful dialogue about some current events that applied to his heritage. I was glad I took the opportunity to get to know him on a more profound level.

A final example is my connection with Samara. She and I worked on several projects together, as she and her team provided oversight. We had interacted for many years but had never taken the chance to get to know one another. I sent her the following email and received a quick reply:

From: Rachel Simon
To: Samara Pelloti
Subject: Lunch one day?

Hi Samara,
Thanks for all the legal advice you have consistently provided to my team! I appreciate how responsive you are. You have helped us to clear some tough roadblocks.

Want to go to lunch one day to get to know each other better? Shame on me that it has taken me this long!

Rachel

From: Samara Pelloti
To: Rachel Simon
Subject: RE: Lunch one day?

I was thinking not too long ago that we should go to lunch. Thanks for taking the initiative to get us together.

Samara

Going to lunch with Samara strengthened our working relationship. We went from casual strangers to collaborators in the time it took us to munch on some chips and salsa. We only had one basket. OK, maybe two, but it was a necessary element to facilitate a meaningful conversation.

READY TO TRY?

Here are some sample emails to get your creative juices flowing. Edit them to fit your own writing style and unique situation.

From: You!
To: Julie Chu
Subject: Meet for coffee?

Hi Julie,
We keep meeting up by the coffee maker on the 14th floor. We seem to be on the same caffeine schedule. ☺ It would be great to get to know you better – want to meet for coffee one day?

From: You!
To: Kevin Crowley
Subject: Lunch one day?

Hi Kevin,
It was good to see you today in our weekly meeting. You did a terrific job on the competitive intelligence presentation and I learned a lot. Want to grab lunch one day to get to know each other better? I think we have a lot in common based on some of the comments I've heard you make!

From: You!
To: Vikram Sirgi
Subject: Hello

Hello Vikram,
It's been such a joy serving on the planning committee for the Employee Day of Caring with you. You have very creative ideas and I can't wait to put it all in motion! I'm surprised our paths hadn't crossed before, but I'm glad they've crossed now. Want to have a virtual cup of coffee one day to get to know each other better? Thanks!

You

From: You!
To: Elijah Fallon
Subject: Get to know you meeting?

Hi Elijah,
It's been really great working on the Vision project for our vice president. I'm glad we were both chosen for this committee and I've learned a lot in the past few months. Mind if I schedule some time for us to chat offline?

From: You!
To: Aidan Miller
Subject: Twin talk over lunch?

Hi Aidan,
It was fabulous to chat with you today while we were waiting for the staff meeting to begin. I didn't realize we both have twins at home that are around the same age. Even though we've seen each other every day for a year, we've never discovered this important point! Want to schedule some time to go to lunch to connect further?

QUESTIONS TO HELP YOU GET STARTED

- Which colleagues do you interact with in meetings who you should get to know better?
- Can you make a list of peers you work with on projects, programs, or committees to connect with for a one-on-one discussion?
- Should you note the people you see daily on your floor whose names you don't even know? Which colleagues do you run into in the hallway or by the water cooler?

- Are you mindful of the people you interact with on an informal basis? Make a list of people you cross paths with daily or weekly.
- How can you hone your mindset to identify opportunities with people around you? How can you shift your thinking that there are people to interact with everywhere?
- How well do you know the people who sit in your immediate vicinity? If approaching someone across the floor scares you, how about the half-dozen people who work right around you?
- Which colleagues do you continually see in virtual meetings or hear on conference calls to connect with offline for a quick follow-up?

TIP 10

Maximize Face-to-Face Time

Not too long ago, I had a meeting with our chief digital officer, who was brand new to the company. Upon reading the announcement of his appointment, I sent a congratulatory email to welcome him. I'm sure it was exciting, yet overwhelming, to join such a big company as a senior manager. I offered to meet to discuss how our teams interacted, and he accepted, genuinely happy that I'd sought him out. In tip 16, I'll discuss the benefits of reaching out when others are new in a job, so I won't belabor the point, but I couldn't resist noting how our initial meeting and subsequent friendship occurred.

The first thing Bala said when I walked into his office was, "You're the DINE! lady!" to which I cheerfully replied, "Yes, I am!" I was very pleased he'd already heard of the initiative I described in tip 4, in which small groups of colleagues come together for vulnerable discussions about their diverse backgrounds. He went on to explain that his job was to digitize operations and remove human contact, which was why, more than ever, we must find ways to *increase* human interaction. After all, what's a world without empathy, warmth, and understanding? What a profound point! As the world becomes more technological, and as we communicate more and more via emails, texts, apps, and social media, we need to seek, cultivate, and foster human connections.

I found myself thinking about our conversation quite a bit. Throughout this book, you can undoubtedly determine my preferred mode of primary communication is email. After all, I've included over two hundred examples for inspiration! The medium is excellent for introverts, as it doesn't require an extraordinary amount of courage to initiate, as opposed to approaching someone for a live conversation. It's an accessible first step to establish and even maintain a relationship. Yet I've discovered that to cultivate and nurture a meaningful connection, face-to-face time can be important.

Upon further objective reflection, I can actually identify a good, better, best tiered strategy for growing reciprocal, authentic connections. While there may not be a single right way to advance a relationship, I've learned there are definitely some tactics that yield a stronger engagement than others.

For example, a *good* mode of keeping in touch with a colleague who lives in another city, or one who works from home, is to send a text or note through a messaging app like WhatsApp, Teams, or Slack. Below is a text I received from Darrell one day:

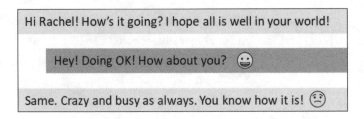

It's certainly good, and I, too, often send this type of "checking-in" text to friends and family scattered across the globe. Texting can be simple and lighthearted, and I've even learned—by necessity—to have full conversations using only emojis, GIFs, and memes. When this text popped up on my device, I smiled and immediately responded. It was quick and easy to reply—almost *too easy*, because there was absolutely nothing significant in the exchange. Still, it served the important purpose of staying connected, and I was grateful to know on that particular day I was on Darrell's mind. It was *good*.

A *better* example would be a more substantive email, like this note I sent to Gretchen, a colleague who worked on my office floor.

From: Rachel Simon
To: Gretchen Mitchell
Subject: Checking in

Hi Gretchen,
Just checking in! Things have been a bit hectic and challenging as I've adjusted to working from home during the pandemic. It took me a few weeks, but I've finally found my groove. I'm grateful that we're safe and healthy and even more thankful that both my husband and I have been able to do our jobs without going to the office. The kids have adjusted to distance learning as well, but they miss their friends. I miss being with people, too! I've now de-cluttered the entire house from top to bottom. I need a hobby, ha! ☺

How have you been? I hope you have remained healthy and work is going OK from home. Has it been difficult or smooth sailing? I miss seeing you!

Rachel

Better, right? While checking in with Gretchen, and letting her know I was thinking of her, I was also able to briefly share how my family was doing. I didn't want the note to be too long—after all, we weren't pen pals, and she didn't need to read a thousand-word essay on the challenges I'd been facing. I received a warm response that maintained our connection, even though we weren't in daily physical proximity anymore.

But the *best* option would be a face-to-face conversation. That's how I've built my network—not email by email, per se, but rather cup of coffee by cup of coffee, conversation by conversation. *Email is simply the vehicle to set the stage for the relationship to progress.* As you've read throughout this book, my ideal next step would be to extend an invitation to grab coffee or lunch. I love meeting one-on-one, where we can have a live conversation to get to know one another or connect in a more substantial way if the relationship already exists. Mentoring relationships in particular are difficult to grow solely via a digital platform. If you've wondered why a desired mentorship has had a failure to launch, perhaps ask yourself if you've used the proper medium. A face-to-face conversation may be precisely what's needed to gain traction.

Yet an in-person, in-the-flesh conversation isn't always possible, especially for those who live in non-headquarters cities or regularly work from home.

Fortunately, technology has advanced to the point that this doesn't necessarily require a physical meet-in-the-same-room presence anymore. It's now common to utilize the multitude of video tools available to look colleagues in the eye, observe their body language, and ensure they— or even you—aren't playing solitaire while having a conversation. An example to get the ball rolling follows:

From: Rachel Simon
To: Marlena Vargas
Subject: Virtual Coffee

Hi Marlena,
I miss seeing you every day in the office! OK if I schedule a virtual coffee for us? Let's have a video chat since we can't get together in person. I thought I'd give you plenty of notice that video is my preference so I don't catch you off guard! Ha. ☺ Let me know your thoughts and I'll get something scheduled.

Rachel

Marlena accepted my invitation, and it was terrific to reconnect. I wasn't bashful in asking for the meeting to be via video. While an audio conversation would still undoubtedly fall into the *best* category, a video conversation for authentic networking purposes is even better. I would call it *bestest*, if that were an everyday word. Also, please note I was proactive in letting her know our meeting would occur via this medium. Those who don't style their hair or forego acceptable office attire while working from home know exactly what I'm talking about!

Many companies periodically hold conferences either for leadership training, sales kickoffs, or general get-togethers. The meetings ensure employees are on the same page to understand the shared mission, vision, priorities, and goals. I view these as prime opportunities to connect with colleagues face-to-face. During the early years of my career, I would leave it to chance to meet coworkers. I'd wander aimlessly around the conference, staring at name tags, then stop someone to say, "Ah! Hi Tim. I'm Rachel. We've worked on projects together. It's good to finally meet you in person!" Over the years, I've become much more deliberate about emailing colleagues in advance I'd like to meet. A few days beforehand, I'll often send an email like this one:

From: Rachel Simon
To: Natalie Sway
Subject: Next week's conference

Hi Natalie,
I'm looking forward to next week's conference! We've been on a zillion calls together but have never met in person. Want to meet up for lunch one day?
Rachel

From: Natalie Sway
To: Rachel Simon
Subject: RE: Next week's conference

Yes! What a great idea! Let's meet outside the far-left ballroom door at 11:30AM for lunch on the first day. Can't wait to connect in person!
Natalie

This email served two equally practical purposes. First, it established a connection with someone I'd never met in person, and it allowed us to strengthen our professional relationship. Second, remember how hard it is for me to walk into a large room of people I don't know? With this email, I secured a lunch partner for the first day and didn't have to enter the dining area alone feeling intimidated and scared. Score!

I also seek out colleagues with whom I may not have the warmest rapports at conferences. Sometimes all it takes is a shared meal in a relaxed environment or a chat during happy hour to change the dynamics of a relationship. At one conference, I saw a colleague across the room with whom I had a strained relationship. I gathered my nerve and joined her while she talked with a few others, as I felt more comfortable in a small group rather than just the two of us. We all had a breezy conversation about the theater—primarily about *Hamilton*, one of my favorite musicals—and it surprisingly moved the needle in our relationship. We learned more about each other personally and shared a few much-needed laughs.

Jason was a member of my team in Missouri, and he traveled once a year to Dallas for a meeting. Before his visit, he sent me the following note:

From: Jason Breck
To: Rachel Simon
Subject: Quick coffee?

Hey Rachel! I know we're going to see lots of each other next week! I'm coming down a day early to meet with some of my team members, and connect with some of my strategic partners face to face.

Just wanted to see if you'd like to get together for a cup of coffee or something on Monday?

Jason

He definitely made the most of his face-to-face time. He was coming to Dallas anyway, but he also scheduled time with various team members and strategic partners, and he proactively asked for thirty minutes with his vice president for coffee.

As another example, Alejandro was a member of my team in El Paso. I was delighted to receive this email:

From: Alejandro Maldova
To: Rachel Simon
Subject: Dallas Trip

Hello Rachel,
Hope you are doing well. I'll be in Dallas in April for a personal trip with my wife and I'd love to get on your calendar for a quick coffee or lunch meeting. I know you're pretty busy but I also wouldn't want to miss an opportunity to have a one-on-one with you. Let me know your availability! Thank you!

Alejandro

It goes without saying he wasn't at all required to visit me on his vacation. But since his work never once took him to company headquarters, he seized the opportunity while in town for personal reasons. I was more than happy to meet with him, and I introduced him to several other colleagues in the building to help him make the most of his time investment.

I've done this before as well. My husband's family lives in New Jersey, and once, while on vacation there after my company had completed a merger, I extended a lunch invitation to my new colleagues. Every single person recognized I didn't have to do that, yet it served to expedite the trust we had in one another and made our relationships that much closer.

I've found that when senior leaders travel to visit centers, factories, or non-headquarters sites, it's often an Event with a capital E. The employees at that location highly anticipate the visit—sometimes with curiosity and trepidation, but usually with pride, as it's a chance to showcase what makes them special and unique. As a result, in jobs in which I had large teams to visit, I always kept this fact in mind and provided plenty of opportunities for them to shine. I structured the day to interact with as many colleagues in person as possible, which typically began with someone picking me up from the airport. I didn't do this to be treated as a high-maintenance VIP—I like to think I'm the opposite—but rather to maximize my time on the ground getting to know a high-potential individual. I discovered long ago that time alone in a rental car was needlessly wasted during these trips. Once at the location, I packed in as many meetings as I could, which ranged from a large town hall–style meeting with Q and A to small group sessions for exploring pressing issues. I often scheduled a DINE! lunch as well with a few select colleagues, and I always carved out time to walk the floor to say hello to each and every employee on my team. My goal was to leave with everyone feeling recognized and special. *Remember: when done properly, networking makes people feel really good.*

If this sounds exhausting for an introvert, the answer is an unequivocal *yes*, it is. I'm absolutely drained by the end of the day! Yet I truly believe that leaders must be visible, especially during a highly anticipated visit that may be a rare event. If at all possible, they shouldn't be tucked away in a conference room the entire day, leaving people to wonder if they were even in the building.

What if you never have the opportunity to travel? What if you work from home? I encourage you to think about who is coming to *your* town, especially if you're not in a headquarters city. It's easy to assume that visitors have their days completely scheduled, but maybe they don't. Here's an email I received from Heather before a trip I made to Los Angeles:

From: Heather Joy
To: Rachel Simon
Subject: Your LA Trip

Hello Rachel, I can't tell you how excited we are that you're coming to LA next week! It's a longshot because I'm sure that every minute of your day is packed, but are you available for a chat while you're here? I would love to pick your brain on a few things in person!

Heather

From: Rachel Simon
To: Heather Joy
Subject: RE: Your LA Trip

Hi Heather, thanks for reaching out! I'd love to get together. My agenda doesn't start until 9AM. Want to meet for coffee at 8:15AM?

Rachel

I was touched that Heather reached out to schedule time with me. I enjoyed getting to know her, and I gained some valuable insights during our coffee session that helped me do my job better.

During a visit to one of my centers in another city, I held an informal group meeting with all managers. It concluded a little bit early, and as everyone filed out of the room, one manager stayed behind and said, "It looks like we ended ten minutes early. Do you mind if I take these ten minutes to chat with you?" Of course! She made the most of the face-to-face time. Furthermore, as I reflected later on the visit, she was the only person who had truly stood out in such a positive, self-motivated way.

As a final example, I received this email from Gino when he heard I was planning a visit relatively close to his work-from-home location:

From: Gino Enigo
To: Rachel Simon
Subject: California visit

Hi Rachel,
I heard you're coming to the Bay Area for a visit and will hold a town hall. I normally telecommute from my home in Sacramento but plan to make the drive for the day and work out of the San Ramon office. I'm looking forward to seeing you in person, since we've had so many conference calls together!

Gino

From: Rachel Simon
To: Gino Enigo
Subject: RE: California visit

Hi Gino, thank you, I am honored! Thank you for making the effort to come when I'm there. I'm looking forward to seeing you as well. Please be sure to come up to introduce yourself!

Rachel

There are endless ways to maximize face-to-face time, whether it's in the flesh or via video. And, of course, if you work for a small company or one that's self-contained in a single location, please utilize all the tips we've discussed to reach out for lunch or coffee with your colleagues. People who work remotely or are spread out from their coworkers might be envious of your proximity to so many in-person opportunities. So don't throw away your shot—I couldn't resist the *Hamilton* reference!

READY TO TRY?

Are you ready to give this tip a try? Here are some sample emails to get your creative juices flowing. Edit them to fit your own writing style and unique situation.

From: You!
To: Leona Craft
Subject: Women's Professional Network in Nashville

Hi Leona,
I heard you're coming to Nashville to speak with the Women's Professional Network. I'll be there and would like to meet for a few minutes to say hello! I'll stay around after the event if you have a few minutes at the conclusion.

I've been a fan of yours from afar for many years and I'm thrilled to get to hear you speak. You've motivated me to achieve many goals in my life and I'd love to share and thank you in person!

From: You!
To: Thalia Rosenberg
Subject: Mentoring Conversation Next Week

Hi Thalia,
Thank you for agreeing to meet with me for a mentoring conversation. I'm looking forward to it – I learn something new every time we speak!

I see we have it scheduled next week on an audio-bridge. Do you mind if I change it to a video meeting? That way we can have a face-to-face conversation even though we are 1,000 miles apart.

From: You!
To: Niles Platt
Subject: Leadership Training Conference

Hi Niles,
I'm in town next week for the Leadership Training conference. Want to meet up for dinner one of the nights? While I'm sure we'll chat about our thorny projects we're working on (GAH!), it will be great just to hang out for a bit and connect. Let me know which night works and we'll plan to meet up!

From: You!
To: Simrin Acoche
Subject: Next week – Philadelphia

Hello Simrin,
I'm coming to our Philadelphia office next month. I have several meetings scheduled throughout the day, but have time in the afternoon if you're available. You're one of my key (and favorite!) clients on the new product launch and I'd love to connect in person. Let me know if that works!

From: You!
To: Landon Williamson
Subject: Breakfast opportunity?

Hello Landon,
I'm looking forward to the summit in NYC that we're both attending. I know we're meeting formally for the first time at 10AM with about a dozen other people. Are you available to meet for breakfast or coffee prior to that? I've heard so many positive things about you and can't wait to put a face to the name – you have an amazing reputation!

From: You!
To: Yen Jong
Subject: Team meeting today – can you join 10 minutes early?

Hi Yen,
We have a team meeting set up via video conference at noon. I'm going to open the bridge a bit early – can you join about 10 minutes beforehand so we can catch up? I would love to chat and see how your family is doing. Thanks!

QUESTIONS TO HELP YOU GET STARTED

- Are you attending a meeting or conference with the opportunity to meet up with colleagues from other cities? Should you send an email in advance to make plans?
- When traveling, is there someone in the same building you are visiting who you should stop in to see? For instance, if you're meeting on the fifteenth floor but have a colleague on the seventh floor not involved in the meeting, can you carve out time so say hello?
- Is a colleague coming to your location? Consider coworkers of all levels and departments who may come to town. Can you ask for a few minutes to meet face-to-face?
- Should you make a list of colleagues located in a city you will be visiting? Would it be beneficial to set aside time to meet with them?
- If you're in a leadership position, how should you structure your day to reach as many people as possible?
- If you're flying into a city for a visit, can you arrange to have someone pick you up from the airport to maximize the connection time on the ground?
- When you visit new locations, who should you go out of your way to meet? Should you schedule group or individual meetings? Should you have meetings over a meal?
- For virtual meetings, do you have opportunities to utilize video rather than audio only? Can you be the person to suggest scheduling the meetings using this medium? Should you open the virtual room early to use the time strategically to chat with a colleague?

TIP 11

Don't Do Any of These Things!

We're at the midpoint of my twenty tips, and subsequently you might be thinking, "Wow, everything comes so easily for her. When she reaches out, she always receives a response, lunches always go hunky-dory, and she's never rejected." Hmm, let's see if I can burst that little bubble.

Believe it or not, every networking relationship I seek doesn't turn to gold. Some turn to solid platinum—those are the best!—and, admittedly, some turn to tin. Or aluminum. Or aluminum foil. Ugh, the worst is when they don't even get off the ground to become aluminum foil. They have a failure to launch, which could be so embarrassing if I let it be. But I don't.

DON'T BECOME DISCOURAGED IF YOU'RE REJECTED

In truth, sometimes I don't receive a response to my emails. My wise stepmom, Jamie, taught me a valuable lesson. She loves to needlepoint, sew, and knit, and has created some beautiful pieces of clothing over the years for my children. I once asked her what I should do with outgrown pieces—did she prefer I hand them down to other cousins, donate them to charity, or keep them as heirlooms? She replied it's entirely up to me what I choose to do. She loves to craft the pieces, and once she snips the last thread, she's done. She enjoys every aspect of the design, the gifting, and the intent behind the creation, and then she's done. She offers it with an open heart and doesn't allow her feelings to be hurt regardless of how it's received or what is done with it after that moment. What a great life lesson in so many ways! I especially relate this insight to sending networking emails. When I write to colleagues to say I enjoyed their speeches or that their leadership style resonates with me, I do so with an open heart. I hope it makes them feel good, and I want them to respond, but I don't allow my feelings to be hurt if they don't. Once I hit the send button, it's gone into cyberspace, and I allow no second-guessing and zero regrets.

Sometimes I write a genuinely thoughtful note, and I don't receive a reply. Gah! How rude, right? In reality, this doesn't happen very often, because *when done properly, networking makes people feel really good*, and it typically elicits a reply. I don't keep track of the no-response emails or glare at the recipients if I don't hear back. I don't feel embarrassed either, as if I did something wrong. And I don't allow myself to become discouraged or stop trying to connect with other colleagues.

Occasionally, however, I do follow up because I wonder if my note was simply lost in an inbox. If your company is anything like mine, we send *a lot* of emails. Like a gazillion a day. It's our culture. I've learned to adapt to the constant flow of information, and I've been able to thrive using email as a tool to establish and maintain many relationships. I do, however, acknowledge that some people struggle mightily to keep up with their inboxes.

I guide my decision to resend a networking email based on a few factors. First, if they exhibit warm behavior toward me, and if it appears that the connection is real, I may hit the send button again. Second, if we must have a strong working relationship, I may try once more, like this example:

From: Rachel Simon
To: Cheri Seebly
Subject: Lunch?

Hi Cheri,
Welcome to the team! Our jobs intersect a lot and we will see each other at multiple meetings throughout the month. I'd love to grab lunch to get to know you better. I can also fill you in on the many projects we are working on and get your opinion on future direction.

Again, welcome and I'm looking forward to working with you!
Rachel

From: Rachel Simon
To: Cheri Seebly
Subject: FWD: Lunch?

Hi Cheri,
It was good to see you today in the calibration meeting - in just a few short months, you've already become a trusted member of the team!

This note may have gotten lost in your email – I know what it's like to start a new job. I'd still love to get lunch if you are open to it! ☺
Rachel

From: Cheri Seebly
To: Rachel Simon
Subject: RE: FWD: Lunch?

Oh my goodness, I am so sorry I never responded to your email!!! Yes, it was crazy in the beginning trying to keep up, but I'm feeling much less overwhelmed now.

YES on lunch. You want to schedule it for sometime next week?
Cheri

I was so glad I reached out to Cheri again. I felt validated to learn my original email was simply overlooked and that our relationship was on the right track. It was the right call to resend it.

DON'T OVERLOOK SIGNS THAT IT MAY BE "ONE-AND-DONE"

Sometimes I have lunch or coffee—in person or virtually—with a colleague, and we talk, laugh, exchange ideas, and the time just flies. We mutually can't believe how quickly the hour went by, and at the end we say to one another, "Let's do this again!" We schedule another lunch a quarter later, and a wonderful relationship is formed. I am fortunate to have a lot of these great connections as I do my part to ensure our time together is full of engaging topics on both a personal and professional level. The dialogue flows easily and I return to my desk happy and fulfilled.

But other times I look at the clock after just five minutes with someone and wonder how on earth I'm going to get through the next fifty-five minutes. I can keep a conversation going with just about anyone for a certain amount of time, but come on, give me *something* to work with! One-word answers and a lack of reciprocal dialogue throw me for a loop and it's hard to partake in a meaningful discussion. I used to feel quite exasperated in these instances. After all, I had the same conversation topics just the day before with someone else—why did this go so terribly wrong? Now I know to refer to these as "one-and-done" sessions. We met once, it wasn't a good match, and we're done. Not every networking meeting is a strong connection. And that's OK!

Chances are high I won't receive any verbal signs to know if a relationship isn't going well. Instead, I must read between the lines. Here's a real example of an exchange I had with a colleague when she needed to reschedule lunch:

From: Charlene Landry
To: Rachel Simon
Subject: Lunch

Hi Rachel!
I just wanted to apologize for being so difficult to schedule lunch with and to thank you for your abundant patience! I see that we're having to move it again for a trip that got booked. I'm so sorry. But I look forward to whenever we ARE able to catch up!
Charlene

From: Rachel Simon
To: Charlene Landry
Subject: RE: Lunch

Hi Charlene,
Thanks for your note! I tell people that I mentor to watch for non-verbal signs to know if a relationship isn't going well – for instance, if she keeps rescheduling lunch, she's just not that into you! So thank you for putting any creeping paranoia at ease! ☺

I'm looking forward to my time with you, so whenever we do see each other, it will be worth the wait. Thanks for the note!
Rachel

From: Rachel Simon
To: Charlene Landry
Subject: RE: Lunch

Oh HA HA HA HA! That really made me laugh! Actually, I always hate to postpone lunches with you because they are so uplifting. I'm overdue for a Rachel fix!
Charlene

It's a funny example, yet I offer it as a genuine tip. Sometimes I schedule lunch with a coworker, and it gets canceled and rescheduled, and canceled and rescheduled, and canceled and rescheduled, and I finally think to myself, *All right, I get the point*, and I don't try again. While it may sting a bit at the moment, I don't take it personally. I just move on. If sometime later she were to say, "Whatever happened to that lunch?" I would take that as my cue to schedule it again.

There is one person in particular who I had the following email exchange with. After lunch was canceled and rescheduled three times, I didn't try again. Here was our original exchange, and I still wonder why it never materialized.

From: Rachel Simon
To: Jill Vicci
Subject: Welcome

Hi Jill,
Congrats on your new role. I've heard terrific things about you and I'm happy that our paths have finally crossed!

Our teams frequently work together so it would be great to get to know you. Do you mind if I schedule coffee or lunch for us?

Rachel

From: Jill Vicci
To: Rachel Simon
Subject: RE: Welcome

Hi Rachel, thank you for the note. Coffee or lunch sounds great so I can learn from you. You can schedule with my assistant.

Jill

There's no written cue to think she didn't want to meet. Why didn't the lunch happen? Maybe she was too busy. Maybe she doesn't go to lunch. Maybe she doesn't value relationships. Maybe she just doesn't like me. I'll never know. I see her in meetings and she has never once mentioned the canceled lunch, nor have I. Instead, I just moved on. This connection just didn't pan out. I can't reiterate enough not to take this rejection personally.

DON'T SEND MASS BLIND-COPIED EMAILS

I've already mentioned how my company utilizes email. We all send and receive a ton. But few people like mass blind-copied emails. They don't inspire action, passion, or emotion in any way and can easily be overlooked as unimportant.

Here is an example of an email I received, although I changed the name to Nata Goodidea.

From: Nata Goodidea
To:
Subject: Happy Holidays!

Season's Greetings!
You have touched my life this year. I want to thank you for the assistance, support, and advice you've given to me. You've been invaluable for my growth and development during this challenging year and I couldn't have gotten through it without you!

Happy holidays to you and your family – wishing you a happy new year!
Nata

It's a nice email, so why am I using it as an example? It's a lovely gesture, filled with gratitude and kind words—except it feels empty and hollow. It's because it was sent blind copied. How many people did it go to? Five? One thousand? I don't know. How many people helped Nata the way that I did this year? Five? One thousand? Again, I don't know. There's no email response to display, because I didn't reply. I simply deleted it. In fact, I should note that I reply to mass blind-copied emails 0 percent of the time. Contrarily, I respond to personal, direct emails 100 percent of the time.

I don't want anyone to think I was annoyed to receive this friendly email. It was nice she thought of me at the holidays. What I'm pointing out, however, is that this is not effective *networking*. Networking would be writing the *same exact* email, then copying and pasting it, and sending it individually to each person. It would look like the email below—it's an identical note, but this time read it through a fresh set of eyes, as if Nata had sent it directly to me and what my probable response would have been.

From: Nata Goodidea
To: Rachel Simon
Subject: Happy Holidays!

Rachel,
Season's Greetings!
You have touched my life this year. I want to thank you for the assistance, support, and advice you've given to me. You've been invaluable for my growth and development during this challenging year and I couldn't have gotten through it without you!

Happy holidays to you and your family – wishing you a happy new year!
Nata

From: Rachel Simon
To: Nata Goodidea
Subject: RE: Happy Holidays!

Nata, wow, what a lovely holiday greeting to receive! It means a lot to me to know that I've touched your life so deeply.

It's been a challenging year, hasn't it? And you have sailed through with flying colors. I'm very proud of you and look forward to seeing what the next year brings. I'm happy to help anytime.

Happy holidays to you and your family as well – what are your plans?
Rachel

Do you see the difference? It was the same exact email but sent individually with my name added. It would have made me feel special, valued, and appreciated. And I'm sure my response would have made her feel great as well. But she never got it, because the second email exchange is fictitious and never occurred.

But wait. You might be thinking, *Does this mean I can never send a blind email to a large group? I must send them individually? That would be ridiculous!* Yes, I agree. If it's simply data or a report that goes to a lot of people, by all means send it blind copied, especially if that's your company culture. In my opinion, however, if the message has even the slightest bit of a personal feel, it should be sent with a viewable distribution list. As an example, here's an email I could have sent following an important meeting that needed a lot of preparation.

From: Rachel Simon
To:
Subject: Meeting today

Team, I know you've been anxiously waiting to hear how the meeting went today...and it went GREAT! THANK YOU so much to each and every one of you for prepping me and making sure I was ready! You all rock – have a restful weekend!

Rachel

I wonder what the recipients would think if they had received this. Probably something along the lines of, *Hmm, how many people had to help Rachel prepare for that meeting? We put in hours and hours and many late nights. Who else helped that we don't know about?* The email feels just a bit off because of the blind-copied nature.

Here's the same exact email, but with the distribution list exposed.

From: Rachel Simon
To: Bob Proctor, Ray Velasquez, Terry Chu, Billie Jones, Van Huang, Sheila Goldstein, Alana Halifa, Grace Simpson
Subject: Meeting today

Team, I know you've been anxiously waiting to hear how the meeting went today...and it went GREAT! THANK YOU so much to each and every one of you for prepping me and making sure I was ready! You all rock – have a restful weekend!

Rachel

It's a small nuance but can make a big difference with networking and showing appreciation.

I'll point out another example that frequently happens. When someone leaves the company, either for retirement or to pursue employment elsewhere, I often receive a mass blind-copied email like the one below. Once again, I don't have a response to this person, because I didn't send one.

From: Chad Johnson
To:
Subject: Last day is tomorrow!

It has been a fabulous 10 years at our company but now it's time for me to start the next chapter of my life. You have been so wonderful to me over the years and I'd love to keep in touch.

My personal email is chadjohnson@poornetworking.com
You can also find me on all social media sites.
Please find me so we can keep in touch!

Chad

It feels so impersonal and must have gone to hundreds of people. I deleted it and went about my day.

Here it is again, reimagined as though Chad had sent the email directly to me and what my likely response would have been.

From: Chad Johnson
To: Rachel Simon
Subject: Last day is tomorrow!

Hi Rachel,
It has been a fabulous 10 years at our company but now it's time for me to start the next chapter of my life. You have been so wonderful to me over the years and I'd love to keep in touch.

My personal email is chadohnson@networking.com
You can also find me on all social media sites.
Please find me so we can keep in touch!

Chad

From: Rachel Simon
To: Chad Johnson
Subject: RE: Last day is tomorrow!

Chad, I'm sorry to see you go! But I am so happy for you! Our Monday meetings won't have the same humor and energy without you. You have been such a terrific partner.

Yes, I will find you on social media and would also love to keep in touch. Best wishes in your new endeavor – what are your plans?

Rachel

The first email was sent to who-knows-how-many-people. The second was the same verbiage, yet it feels personal, simply by calling me by my name. It would have made me feel honored that he thought to send me an individual email informing me that he was moving on. I hope you can see the difference between the two approaches to achieve maximum networking benefits.

DON'T ASK FOR TOO MUCH

By now you know I'm encouraging you to be brave and bold and reach out to colleagues to schedule time to get to know them. But there is such a thing as being too brave and too bold and overstepping. It's a fine line, and let's be honest—the line is different for everyone. Therefore, it's important not to ask for too much.

I received the following email from a colleague. I was delighted to get his note telling me that he watched my presentation. But then my delight soured a bit when I discovered how much he was asking from me right off the bat.

From: Kory Little
To: Rachel Simon
Subject: Mentoring

Hi Rachel,
I saw your presentation that you gave recently on career tips. I was wondering if you would have time to mentor me for six months? 30-45 minutes a month would be ideal.

I have attached my resume for review and I'm looking forward to hearing from you so we can begin our mentoring relationship.

Thank you very much.

Kory

From: Rachel Simon
To: Kory Little
Subject: RE: Mentoring

Hi Kory,
Thanks for reaching out! I'm glad you were able to watch my presentation and that you enjoyed it. Hopefully you got a nugget or two that will help you in the future.

Why don't you schedule a one-time 30-minute session for us to get to know each other? My calendar is up to date.

Looking forward to it.

Rachel

I love mentoring and get a lot out of it, but the best relationships happen organically. I had no idea what to expect from Kory and didn't want to commit too much up front, which could have led to resentment down the line and dreading our time together if it wasn't a good match. Sure enough, this was a one-and-done. He didn't come prepared for the discussion with any thoughtful questions, and the thirty-minute session lasted only about fifteen minutes. I was relieved I hadn't committed more time without knowing him. He was a bright man and a true asset to the company, but we just weren't a good match.

Because I've done this a lot, I had the skill to pivot his request of six months at thirty to forty-five minutes each to a one-time session without hurting his feelings. But many others may not have reacted as kindly. Some may have deleted the request because of the overask, while others may have responded with a gentle—or not-so-gentle—no.

Also, be sure to read the signs regarding the frequency of interaction. A few years ago, I had coffee with a new employee, Mitch. It was a pleasant meeting, and we both enjoyed it. At the end, he said, "This was fantastic. Can we do this again in a couple of weeks?" Ugh. That's asking for too much. I cheerfully replied, "Meeting again in a few months sounds great!" I didn't apologize that I couldn't meet sooner or muster a lame excuse. Thankfully, he read between the lines and appropriately scheduled coffee again the next quarter without me needing to be more blatant.

The moral of this tip is not to ask for too much. It puts the receiver in the awkward position of saying no and sets up the sender to feel embarrassed. The best way to avoid this is to ask for a *one-time* coffee, lunch, virtual meeting, etc., and see where it goes.

READY TO TRY?

Are you ready to give these tips a try? That was a trick question—*don't do any of these*! The title of the chapter, after all, is "Don't Do Any of These Things!" I'm making sure you are paying attention, which undoubtedly you are.

Nonetheless, here is some verbiage if you need to resend an email you believe may have been overlooked. Be sure to edit it to fit your own writing style and unique situation.

From: You!
To: Ashley O'Leary
Subject: Introduction

Hi Ashley,
I'm new to my role in business marketing and would really appreciate the opportunity to come by to meet you. I've heard your name many times since I've been here and I'd love to pick your brain about new ideas for partnership.

OK to schedule some time?

From: You! (Resend)
To: Ashley O'Leary
Subject: FWD: Introduction

Hi Ashley,
Just following up on this request – I'd truly appreciate having a few minutes to sit down and chat.

I know you're busy, so thank you for the consideration!

Here is some verbiage to use if you are the one in the position in which someone is asking too much of *you*:

From: Keith Quintos
To: You!
Subject: Serve on a committee?

We've never met, but I've heard you'd be a good person to serve on a committee for our newly-formed Employee Group. We meet once a month and could use your expertise. Is this something you can do?

Keith

From: You!
To: Keith Quintos
Subject: RE: Serve on committee?

Hi Keith,
Thank you for your email and for your faith in my abilities! Serving on a new committee just isn't in the cards right now with other obligations I've taken on. I wish you the best with your Employee Group.

You

QUESTIONS TO HELP YOU GET STARTED

- Is there someone you didn't receive a response from who you should resend an email?

- Do you need to read between the lines regarding a relationship that may have fizzled? Do you need to move on?

- Are you sending mass blind-copied emails that need to be personalized?

- Are you asking for too much when you reach out? Do you need to dial down your requests and expectations?

- Have you noticed a pattern of negative responses to your requests that may cause you to reconsider your approach or verbiage? Are you using the right medium?

- Have you let a negative experience in the past hold you back from reaching out to new people? How can you put that behind you to try again?
- Do you need to consider the timing of your emails to elicit a better answer? For instance, sending a note at the end of the quarter or before an important deadline may not evoke a favorable reply if stress is running high.
- Do you have a realistic expectation of when you should expect to hear back to your requests?
- Can you reflect on emails you've received that may have been off-putting? What about them was poorly worded that didn't inspire action? How could you learn from those so as not to make similar mistakes when you reach out to colleagues?

TIP 12

Write Thank-You Notes

There's a saying, "Actions speak louder than words," and while often true, I also know how much words matter. Words can be used to lift people up or push them down, to bring out the best in people, or to make them feel worthless. I've been on the receiving end of both, and I know which I prefer. There are supervisors and colleagues I would line up around the block to have the chance to work with, and the one trait they all have in common is that they show their sincere appreciation. They are generous with their praise, feedback, and gratitude.

I'm not sure there's anyone who doesn't welcome a thank-you note, and I can't think of a single instance when I've thought to myself, *I wish he hadn't taken the time to thank me.* At its worst, a thank-you note can be perceived as neutral, while at its best it could change the warmth of a relationship and pay untold dividends down the road. Appreciation inspires higher performance and taps into our natural human desire to receive recognition for our efforts. The quickest way to add a spring in someone's step or have her walk just a bit taller is to show gratitude, and I've learned it's absolutely critical in the workplace.

My colleague Cathy once gave me some solid advice. She said, "Rachel, when you send a thank-you note, make sure it's personal enough that you can't just substitute one person's name for another." For instance, don't write a note saying, "Thank you for your presentation." Instead, a better version would be, "Thank you for your presentation. Here's what I got out of it." Then proceed to detail the specifics. The difference is clear: the first is generic; the second is specific. The first one is nice to receive, while the latter is impressive.

This piece of excellent advice is something I put into practice every time I pause to thank someone. I ask myself, "How can I be specific? How will they be delighted that I noticed their efforts?"

I wrote this email to Maya, one of my colleagues who had a knack for knowing exactly how to help the whole team, me in particular:

From: Rachel Simon
To: Maya Lupito
Subject: Thank you!

Hi Maya,
I didn't want the week to end without stopping to tell you how much I appreciate you! You are doing such an amazing job supporting our team which makes us all SHINE! The team has told me on multiple occasions that they feel informed and up to date on deadlines.

In addition, you know the right things to do and say to get me to smile during a stressful day – and you know the exact moments I need chocolate to push through! ☺

I really do appreciate you and I'm so grateful we get to work together. Thank you!

Rachel

I came in the next day to a piece of homemade chocolate cake from Maya. Perhaps it was a happy coincidence, but I believe she appreciated the heartfelt note and wanted to reciprocate the thanks. And wow, was it delicious.

I also periodically ask my colleagues to tell me who has done an exceptional job. I simply inquire, "Who should I thank for their efforts?" Once I receive a list, I drop a quick, informal yet individual note of thanks for their efforts, like the one below:

From: Rachel Simon
To: Robert Pooley
Subject: Thank you!

Hi Robert,
Lisa has told me what an incredible job you're doing for our team. These are challenging times and you've ramped up your knowledge to create the new reports we need. The reports are clear and easy to read – they will definitely drive the action we're looking for.

I appreciate all the hours you're pouring into making sure we're successful. I know it's tough to balance it all right now, and you're doing an unbelievable job... with your trademark can-do personality as well.

Thank you!
Rachel

My emails are typically met with enthusiasm and possess a general tone of humility. They usually state that, while they are glad to help, they are just doing their jobs. Yet they are grateful I noticed their efforts. Those are my favorite thank you notes to send—when they're not expected and therefore truly brighten up an inbox.

I've received some lovely thank-you notes over the years as well, which illustrate the point of specificity. For example, I received this email from Shane, an engaged participant in one of my mentoring circles:

> **From:** Shane Middleton
> **To:** Rachel Simon
> **Subject:** Thank you!
>
> Hi Rachel,
> Thank you very much for being our mentor over the past year through our mentoring circle. I learned a lot through your presentations but also in your demeanor and how you treat others. You're very authentic and relatable and that makes you very unique.
>
> I think my two favorite presentations were our personal brand statements and resume review. I now have a perfect resume ready to go at any time thanks to you. It was great to gain insight into your life and work and I can't thank you enough for sharing all of that.
>
> Thanks for everything you've done to help me be successful!
> *Shane*

Shane's email was genuine and specific about the two lessons he learned from me instead of just a bland "thank-you." It was also a helpful email, as I noted his feedback of which topics were ones I should continue in future circles.

Not long ago, I spoke to a group of employees as their keynote speaker, and the following day I received this email from the organizer:

> **From:** Vance Parker
> **To:** Rachel Simon
> **Subject:** Thank you for your speech yesterday!
>
> Hi Rachel,
> Thank you for taking the time to be our keynote speaker for the leadership program kickoff. Your message for our mentees was very inspiring. Your five core mentoring principles listed below align with our program and resonated with all of us. I took notes! 1) Be curious and ask questions 2) Ask for feedback 3) Make leadership proud 4) Be authentic and true to yourself 5) Implement best practices. Thanks again and I'm excited to be part of your team!
> *Vance*

Vance's note of appreciation was fantastic. Not only did it close the loop, as I participated at his request, but he showed that he paid attention to my speech and valued my time. I was impressed!

Several years ago, I was asked to be a speaker at an event about interviewing skills. The next day I received this email from Elaine, thanking me for my time:

From: Elaine Lansing
To: Rachel Simon
Subject: Thank you for your time yesterday

Hi Rachel!
Thank you for the useful interview tips you shared during the Women of Finance event yesterday. I learned a lot and appreciate that you spent the time. I had a meeting scheduled right after so I didn't have time to stay and ask you a question. I'm wondering if it would be okay to ask the interviewer to introduce me to the team or even the person who did the job before? I'd like to get some ideas before taking the job. The best info probably comes from people who did it before, but I'm not sure if it's too soon to bring it up during the first interview.

Would appreciate your comments, thanks!
Elaine

Elaine's email was really well done. She expressed her appreciation—the only one to do so out of about eighty people—and she provided an excellent example of the two-way communication I've referenced. She asked a thoughtful question, I responded with a thoughtful answer, and we agreed to chat over lunch. Our relationship blossomed, and it all started with this email thank-you note.

As I shared in tip 10, I make it a priority to visit employees on my team in various locations around the globe. I put a lot of effort into the visits, as it's important that they're personable, warm, and engaging, while also focused on results and accountability. I felt like I hit the mark after receiving this note from Elliott:

From: Elliott Higgs
To: Rachel Simon
Subject: Thank you for the visit!

Rachel, I wanted to take a minute to say thank you for the visit you made to our location. The center was thrilled to see you again. I know I've said this before, but it's great to have a leader who makes the time to visit our operations and shows appreciation for our hard-working employees. They especially liked the town hall format and the session you did on networking skills. I hope you enjoyed the rest of your weekend and I'll see you soon!

Elliott

I visited with hundreds of people that day, but only Elliott took the time to send an email letting me know the trip was a success. He certainly stood out in my mind.

I received the following email from Laura. We had gotten to know each other over the course of two years, and her unexpected words touched me.

From: Laura Inalgo
To: Rachel Simon
Subject: Thank you

Rachel,
You have made a tremendous difference to my growth as a leader and I wanted to say thank you. You have shown how to be compassionate, set clear expectations, work up and down every chain, and make a difference in the world with grace and humor. You let us get to know you and you take the time to get to know us. I have soaked in the experiences I have had with you and made them part of my fabric. Thanks so much for your leadership!

Laura

Wow, that was a keeper of an email! It made me feel on top of the world to know my leadership had made a difference and that I exhibited so many important attributes. *Remember: when done properly, networking makes people feel really good.* Perhaps there's someone in your life to send a similar note that would make their day.

During a time of reorganization, I was happy to receive the following note from Yolanda after she received some new responsibilities on our team. Her supervisor and I had been very deliberate about choosing her for a new role, as we thought she had the perfect skills to take it on, but we understood her possible trepidation of leaving a place of comfort.

From: Yolanda Gonzalez
To: Rachel Simon
Subject: Thank you!

Rachel,
Thanks again for the opportunity to add another stop to my journey with the team. I've learned so much in each of my roles and I'm really excited to find out what this one has in store for me. I've realized that embracing being uncomfortable and continuously raising my hand for projects have given me the opportunity to gain skills and grow as a leader.

I enjoy being involved in different things and will continue to raise my hand for opportunities to take on projects and/or additional responsibilities. We are only as successful as our team, so I'm here to do whatever I can to help with the success.

Yolanda

Her thoughtful email made me feel at ease with the decisions that occurred during that time period, and I appreciated it very much.

There are endless amounts of verbiage to use when writing a sincere thank-you note. Here are twenty examples to get you thinking:

1. Thanks for meeting with me today.

2. Thank you for everything you do for me.

3. I appreciate you so very much.

4. I can always count on you.

5. Thank you for the energy and passion you bring to work every day.

6. Thank you for being such an amazing colleague.

7. You always seem to drop everything to help me.

8. Your help with this project is so appreciated.

9. Thanks for your inspirational leadership.

10. You always lead by example, and I want to say thank you.

11. It's a joy and privilege to be a part of your team.

12. Thank you for the extra project, which allowed me to shine.

13. I'm grateful for your dedication.

14. Thank you for believing in me.

15. Thank you for coaching me.

16. Thank you for putting in extra time and effort to help me.

17. Thank you for your flexibility and willingness to work with me on this issue.

18. Your hard work doesn't go unnoticed.

19. I want to express my gratitude for being such a wonderful colleague and friend.

20. Thank you for always going above and beyond to ensure the success of a project.

People respond to appreciation differently, and it's essential to learn to express it in the most meaningful way *to the receiver*. Sure, it's easy to send a blanket email to say thank you, and to be clear, that's absolutely better than nothing. But for others, how could you tap into the manner in which they prefer to receive praise? Perhaps it's copying their supervisor on a thank-you email. Maybe it's public recognition in front of others, either formally or informally. Possibly it's treating them to lunch or a cup of coffee. At one point of my career, I kept a stack of gift cards to the local coffee shop and sent them to coworkers who went out of their way to assist me. As I've already mentioned, a few colleagues over the years have gifted me with sweets as a way of showing their thanks—yes, it's a well-known fact I love chocolate! One person sent me a fruit basket—OK, maybe it's *not* a well-known fact I love chocolate!—and a few have sent me flowers as gratitude for something extra I did. These gifts were unnecessary for sure, but I can tell you that they added a bold exclamation mark to the appreciation they were offering. They made an impact. There are endless creative ways to express thanks, but the key point is to express it in a way that's valued by the receiver.

During a hectic time of year for my team, I sent this note to Caleb and took the opportunity to copy his boss, as I thought it would be meaningful to praise him in front of his supervisor.

From: Rachel Simon
To: Caleb Johansson
CC: Caleb Johansson's Boss
Subject: Thank you!

Caleb,
I know you've been carrying a heavy load recently – between budget and strategy, all roads seem to go through you! I want to make sure you know how much I appreciate you and I'd like to take you to lunch. As tough as things are, you make it a lot easier for me. Have a great weekend!

Rachel

From: Caleb Johansson
To: Rachel Simon
CC: Caleb Johansson's Boss
Subject: RE: Thank you!

Thanks for the note, Rachel! I greatly appreciate it. We have a good team and we will not only get through this tough time, but I believe we'll come out even better than we were before. Would love to go to lunch – thanks!

Caleb

I'm frequently asked about whether a handwritten or digital note is best. Let me first answer it this way: you be you. If you prefer sending handwritten thank-you notes, then that's what you ought to do. If your mother would never forgive you for not mailing one, or if you think a handwritten note would differentiate your gratitude within a sea of emails and texts, by all means do that! There's no wrong way to send a note of appreciation, as long as it's sincere and individualized. But as far as my personal preference goes, I like a digital note because I enjoy the two-way communication that often comes with it. A great example is below:

From: Rachel Simon
To: Andrea Segovian
Subject: Thank you!

Andrea,
Thank you so much for your help today in prepping for the project readout. Your presentation skills are incredible and my slides look amazing now! Thank you for taking the time, I appreciate you. YOU ROCK!
Rachel

From: Rachel Simon
To: Andrea Segovian
Subject: RE: Thank you!

Wow, Rachel, I wasn't expecting to get such a nice note. I was just doing my job which I love ☺. It's a pleasure to work with you.
Andrea

Not only did Andrea feel great about my appreciation but her response expressing *her* appreciation of *my* appreciation made *me* feel great! It was a beautiful loop I would have missed if I had sent a handwritten note.

And yet, when done the right way, a handwritten note may be exactly what's called for. I received the most beautiful card from my colleague, Chloe, after she received a promotion.

Hi Rachel,

Seldom do life-changing people come around in your life – I am so incredibly fortunate to have met such a shining example of one – you! The day you approached me and asked to get to know me a bit better will remain forever in my fond memories. You saw something in me that I had not seen in myself. I would be remiss if I didn't take a moment to acknowledge and appreciate you for all you've done for me. Not only have you been an excellent role model, mentor, and counselor, but you've also been a strong advocate (and that is not lost on me). I am overjoyed to be embarking on this new journey in my career and I have you to thank for helping me get here. Thank you from the bottom of my heart for all you've done to enrich my life!

With sincere gratitude,
Chloe

Wow! This card was so touching. I picked up the phone to call Chloe to thank her for her meaningful words. From the time this card was written to the present day, our relationship has grown stronger in every way possible: networking, mentoring, and friendship. Perhaps Chloe's touching words will inspire you to send a similar heartfelt note to someone who has meant a lot to you.

Have you ever thought about sending a thank-you note to your supervisor after a glowing appraisal or pay raise? I hadn't either, until I received this email from Bill:

From: Bill Runford
To: Rachel Simon
Subject: Thank you

Rachel,
I don't want the week to end without saying Thank You for the rating and related compensation. It means a lot to be recognized in this way.

I appreciate the investment and will continue to exceed your expectations and make you proud. I'm very happy to be in this organization and to work with such a great leadership team. I learn and grow everyday and enjoy working with our constituents... all which keeps my skills sharp and makes each day an exciting challenge.

Thanks again – I won't let you down!
Bill

Bill earned the high rating and every dollar of his pay raise, and the thank-you note was quite superfluous. Yet it was extremely thoughtful and made me smile.

Writing a thank-you note may be one of the easiest, most worthwhile tips in the book to execute. It costs nothing and is almost guaranteed to brighten someone's day, especially if it's sent out of the blue. You can even add clip art of virtual flowers, a cute GIF, music, or other creative gestures to make the email stand out. Just remember to be authentic and for your words and actions to consistently align!

READY TO TRY?

Are you ready to give this tip a try? Here are some sample emails to get your creative juices flowing. Edit them to fit your own writing style and unique situation.

From: You!
To: Louisa Thompson
Subject: Thank you!

Louisa,
I just wanted to drop you a note to say thank you for being such an inspirational person in my life. There are many times I find myself quoting you when I'm talking to others. You're one of the few people who cares just as much about people as you do about results.

I'm grateful to work on your team and look forward to relaying many more words of wisdom. Thank you for being you!

From: You!
To: Mayumi Liu
Subject: Thank you!

Mayumi,
Thank you for the great webcast town hall you hosted! The team is buzzing with positive feedback. You delivered a great portrayal of the state of the business and the challenges we have, but with optimism and excitement. I'm thrilled to be part of your team!

From: You!
To: Fred Hutchins
Subject: Thank you so much

Hello Fred,
I wanted to thank you for attending the staff meeting in my absence today as I was double-booked. And furthermore, thank you for taking such good notes to share with me. The summary you provided was fantastic. I really appreciate it and I'm grateful for your partnership.

From: You!
To: Mariana Oliveta
Subject: Thank you

Mariana,
I just left the big presentation and there wasn't a single question I couldn't answer. Your hard work on producing the deck made all the difference. I know you and the team spent many late hours preparing the slides and I just wanted to say thank you for the excellent effort and attention to detail. Next cup of coffee is on me – I dropped a small gift card in the mail.

From: You!
To: Monique Ibotta
Subject: Thank you for the excellent review and pay raise!

Monique,
I shared with my partner tonight about the excellent review and commiserate pay raise you gave me. I told him how appreciative I was. He asked if I had told YOU that... good point!

Thank you so much for taking the time to document my many accomplishments. It was the most well-thought out review I've ever received. I had a great year and I feel very valued in my position – thank you for making me feel that way. You are an amazing boss. Have a great evening!

You

From: You!
To: Sinead O'Malley and Jackson Willis
Subject: Thank you for the attention to detail!

Sinead and Jackson,
Thank you to the best tech team ever! I would have been lost without you today giving my speech. From the moment you attached the microphone to my lapel to the way you connected the live presentation to the virtual audience online, everything was smooth and seamless. I know sometimes the behind-the-scenes work is not noticed, so that's why I especially want to stop and recognize you for your hard work. Thank you so much!

From: You!
To: Kai Lee
Subject: Thank you so much for your time today

Kai,
You did such an amazing job presenting at my staff meeting about personal branding. You spoke with passion, purpose, and warmth – your energy was contagious! You gave everyone a lot to think about, especially about how their personal brands play into who they are and who they aspire to be. There was such a fabulous buzz in the air after you left.

I truly appreciate you taking the time. Thank you!

QUESTIONS TO HELP YOU GET STARTED

- Who has helped you with your work? To whom should you offer appreciation?
- Who has visited your work location or given a speech you admired that you should thank?
- How can you elevate your writing to be specific with your gratitude?

- How can you thank someone in the manner in which they want to be acknowledged, such as a public forum?
- How can you use thank-you notes to provide exposure? Should you copy their boss or others in their chain of command?
- Should you build fifteen minutes into your schedule at the end of your week to write thank-you notes, or should you write them as you go along?
- What are the key milestones of a project for which you can express thanks? You don't need to wait until a project is complete to offer gratitude.
- When were times you worked hard that you wish you'd received recognition? Remember that feeling the next time you're in a position to express your gratitude.

TIP 13

Utilize Your Network to Secure a New Position

Throughout my career, I've been on many interviews for jobs I've applied for, and, as you may recall, I never was offered any of them. Not a single one. Why is that? Since I think of myself as an articulate communicator and a reasonably strong interviewee, something else must have gone dreadfully wrong either before, during, or after the interview. Early on, it might have been my lack of experience, as I competed for positions against highly tenured employees. Before my confidence ratcheted up, it might have been that I didn't appear self-assured. I might have come across as too meek, too mild mannered, or too unprepared for the job, even if I was more than ready. Once, it might have been that I didn't send a thank-you note to the hiring manager after an interview. It still haunts me to this day that I didn't send him a note of appreciation for his time, and I even have an occasional nightmare about it! Who really knows why I didn't get any of those jobs? But you can tell I've reflected on this subject. A lot.

But maybe it was something else. Perhaps something didn't go *wrong* for me but instead went *right* for someone else. You've undoubtedly heard the saying, "It's who you know." I've always despised that phrase. For me, it conjures up images of a privileged, unreachable network I could never tap into, no matter how hard I worked. My colleague, Mark, expanded upon the concept in the most liberating way and explained, "Everyone thinks it's who you know, but it's actually the opposite—it's *who knows you*." Ah, so profound! Saying that I know so-and-so-big-shot is not enough. It's a paradigm shift to reconsider the idea that they need to know *me*. They need to know my skills and capabilities, and furthermore, they need to be willing to recommend me to others. I need to be the type of person for whom they would put their solid-gold reputations on the line to advance my career. Perhaps the people who earned the jobs I was rejected from had colleagues, supervisors, or others in their network who were willing to do this for them.

To further answer my own question of what went right for everyone else, I need only to consider what I personally contemplate when I'm the hiring manager. At my company, job openings are posted on an internal company-wide site. I typically receive dozens of applicants and it's important that I consider a well-rounded diverse slate of candidates. What advances someone to the interview stage with me? Since I assume the list of candidates wouldn't have made it through the human resources screening process if they weren't all qualified, it essentially comes down to two decision points.

First, to secure an interview with me, a well-prepared résumé is a must. Applicants won't get an interview because they have a *great* résumé, but they most certainly could lose an interview opportunity because they have a *bad* résumé. Does that make sense? If it's thorough and packed with accomplishments and skill qualifications, it's considered table stakes and what I expect from a competent employee. But if the résumé is full of typos and grammatical errors, I simply cannot get past that oversight. If this is how they put their best foot forward when they have all the time in the world to prepare, how would they handle themselves in crunch time? Sorry, no interview. At this point, I hope a lot of you are scrambling to dust off your résumés to see if they need a refresh. You have complete control of what you decide to include, and it falls on no one else's shoulders but your own.

I will leave it at that because this book is not about building an impeccable résumé, but I implore you to ensure it's in flawless, up-to-date condition. If you were requested at 4:55 p.m. to submit for your dream job that day by 5:00 p.m., would it be ready? Add this to your priority to-do list if the answer is no—please read this in the nagging voice that I intend!

Second, I focus on who is recommending the applicant, which means everything to me. Who can speak on his behalf? Who can tell me about the impressive turnaround that she did in her last role? Who can share that he's ready to take on a new daunting task with many buried political land mines? Who can convince me that though I may be tempted to cast her résumé aside because she doesn't appear to have a ton of experience, she has soared in every role she's ever taken? Who can explain that this person is a diamond in the rough and that with proper development will shine brighter than anyone else I've ever worked with in the past?

I can't glean this type of intelligence from a résumé, and although I may be able to tease out this information in an interview, I need it *beforehand* to whittle down who even gets to that stage. I need this knowledge to ensure I choose the right person for the job, as there is simply too much at stake to make a poor hiring decision.

As you can likely surmise, I gather this type of information by using my network to assemble the best slate of diverse candidates. I do this in several ways.

First, I think about who I personally know who may be a good fit for the open role. Of course, I consider my current team to assess if anyone may be ready for a promotion or a lateral job rotation. But I also think about past experiences and interactions; for example, I selected Pam based on our previous working relationship when she excelled, and I promoted Tiffany based solely on what I watched her accomplish with the Women of Finance. The positive experiences with both of them in the past proved to be exactly what I needed to assess future opportunities.

Next, I ask my colleagues if there is anyone in their networks they should encourage to apply for the open role. I have a few reliable peers whose judgment I trust to send me superstars who might not be on my radar but have the specific skills I need.

Finally, I seek the opinion of trusted colleagues who might know the top applicants I'm considering. I reach out proactively for insights and a solid thumbs-up or thumbs-down. Do their eyes light up when I mention a candidate's name?

It's a consistent practice of mine to reach out to colleagues when I need their opinions on candidates. But as a hiring manager, it's even better when the knowledge comes directly to me in the form of a personal recommendation. It reveals a lot about the candidates that they want the job enough to call upon their network to speak on their behalf. For example, I received this email from a peer when I was seeking a new manager on my team:

From: Pierce Kogan
To: Rachel Simon
Subject: Recommendation – Jana Bollagio

Hi Rachel,
A colleague of mine has applied for an open position on your team. Jana Bollagio is such a terrific co-worker. She's inquisitive, upbeat, and has an amazing work ethic. She has recently completed her bachelor's degree and is ready for a role in management. I'd hire her myself if I had an opening.

I attached her resume. Would you please give some consideration to interviewing her? I'd appreciate it.

Pierce

I was delighted to give Jana an interview based solely on the recommendation from a peer. Her résumé might have been easily overlooked because of her lack of specific experience, but it rose to the surface once I received this email.

A few years ago, I got to know Brian when we collaborated on a committee. I was quite impressed with him and the energy he brought to the team, and we maintained our relationship once the committee disbanded. I was pleased when I received this note asking me to advocate for him as he applied for a new role within the company:

From: Brian Needles
To: Rachel Simon
Subject: Favor

Rachel,
You told me once that if you could ever lend a hand in helping me to get a new opportunity to make sure I reached out to you. I promised you I would take advantage of that incredible offer before long. I have been nominated for an assignment in the credit department.

A few key skills that I possess that you could speak to would be:
- Communication skills
- Organization
- Adaptation to new technology
- Project management and follow through

Thank you for any assistance you can provide. I consider you to be an incredible leader and I feel fortunate that I can call on you as a personal brand advocate for me!
Brian

Let me tell you how much I love Brian's email. It had all the elements of receiving an affirmative response. He explained why he was reaching out, flattered me—*remember: when done properly, networking makes people feel really good*—and outlined his skills. I didn't have to scratch my head and think, *What do I know about Brian?* He made it so easy for me, as he laid it all out. I was more than happy to write a letter of recommendation, and he did get the job—not because I wrote a note, but *it didn't hurt*. A personal letter of recommendation can make all the difference to a hiring manager.

I offer two words of caution when asking people to write you glowing letters of recommendation: First, make sure it's a job you genuinely want. If you're applying for a new role every other day and calling upon your network each time, I assure you it's going to get old at a very swift pace. Think carefully to respect your networks' time. Second, make sure the person you're asking to speak on your behalf has a good reputation. I once received a note from someone who had a terrible reputation, which made me wonder if the applicant exhibited questionable judgment!

Jwyanza told me about a role he applied for and asked me to send a note to the hiring manager. I was happy to write the following email:

From: Rachel Simon
To: Gary Fields
Subject: Recommendation – Jwyanza Wells

Hi Gary,
Jwyanza has applied for your open Assistant Vice President role and I would appreciate it if you would grant him an interview. Although he has never been in my organization, I've gotten to know him through the finance diversity and inclusion council, where he was a standout. He's passionate about this topic and about paying it forward.

I can't say enough good things about him, but I will try... he's a hard worker with high integrity and a quality individual who is considerate, respectful, and caring to those around him. He's appreciative, easy to get along with, diligent, and hard working. These are traits that have served him well in finance and would be an asset to your organization.

I'd consider it a favor if you would interview him – then the rest is up to him!
Rachel

Jwyanza was thankful I took the time to send a letter of recommendation, and he did indeed obtain an interview. Gary was also appreciative that I went out of my way to endorse a top-performing employee when I had nothing to gain from the interaction.

How should you choose individuals to be a referral for you? Naturally, you would ask yourself, "Who do I know that knows the hiring manager?" It's great if you have a list of several colleagues to choose from, but you only really need one. Attaining twenty letters of recommendation from twenty different people is not necessary and is frankly overdoing it. But it needs to be the right one, so choose wisely. Once you have your list, select the person who sincerely knows your expertise, talents, and what you have to offer. Don't automatically select the highest-level person on the list, although that may prove to be a smart route. Some companies are very hierarchical, and if you think that's the best approach, then go for it. Just remember that the recommender is only helping to position you for an interview. It's great if a senior manager recommends you for an interview, but you need to ace it and earn the job on your own merit.

Be sure to attach your résumé to your request and give the recommender plenty of time. I once had someone ask me for a letter of recommendation the night before it was due. I was pretty annoyed—OK, a lot annoyed—and I had to consider if I would write it. Ultimately, I decided that yes, I would, because it was an excellent opportunity for her, and she herself hadn't been given a ton of notice. While the urgency added a burden on me that I decided to overlook, I wonder how many other people would have or could have done it with such little notice. My guess is not many; therefore be sure to provide as much time as possible when asking someone to do you a favor. Be detailed in your request about your timeline and the due date.

Sometimes it's inevitable that multiple job opportunities present themselves in quick succession within a short period of time, and you may need to ask for repeated help from one particular supporter. In the email below, I like how Carol got ahead of this by sending me a proactive note.

From: Carol Lanarro
To: Rachel Simon
Subject: Your advocacy

Hi Rachel,
I know I've called on you a lot recently to speak on my behalf and I want you to know how much I appreciate you! Having your endorsement for a job means the difference between being considered and not being considered. I hope it's OK to continue to call on you as I see roles that align with my skills and passions.

Your support means the world to me – thank you!

Carol

Her email acknowledged that I've gone to bat for her multiple times and prepared me that I may be asked to do it again. If you're considering using this type of email, it may be the perfect opportunity to send a small gift card to the local coffee shop as a thank you, like we discussed in tip 10.

It's also important to close the loop one way or another when you ask someone to be a referral. I was over the moon to receive this email from Shaka when she was promoted to a new position:

From: Shaka Abebe
To: Rachel Simon
Subject: Your recommendation!

Rachel,
I wanted to follow up and thank you for calling Cathy to recommend me for the director job. When I asked you to be a reference, you came through big time! In the interview, Cathy raved about you (we are both mutual fans of yours, so that was easy) and she told me the nice things that you said about me. In fact, she said that you said, "If you don't hire Shaka, you are really missing out!" ☺

All that is to say that I got the promotion and I owe that to you!!! I wanted you to be the first to know. THANK YOU so much. I would like to treat you to lunch to thank you properly. Your support means so much to me.
Shaka

From: Rachel Simon
To: Shaka Abebe
Subject: RE: Your recommendation!

Aw, Shaka, this email makes me extraordinarily happy! I AM SO PROUD OF YOU! It's easy to advocate for great people and that is you! ☺

Yes, we will absolutely go to lunch to celebrate your big promotion!
Rachel

I would have heard about her promotion at some point, but the fact that she sent me such a joyful, appreciative note made me feel elated. I did tell the hiring manager that she would be missing out if she didn't hire Shaka, and I'm glad those powerful words of endorsement appeared to help.

Here's another example of closing the loop. I'm sure it was hard for Alex to send me this email to tell me that he didn't get the job, as he would have preferred to send me exciting news of a promotion.

From:	Alex Klein
To:	Rachel Simon
Subject:	Job interview follow up

Hi Rachel,
Thank you very much for serving as a reference for me when I applied for the role under Ken. Unfortunately, I found out today that I didn't get the job.

Of course I'm disappointed, but I'm grateful that I had the opportunity to interview and that was probably because you put in a good word for me.

My goal is still to earn a promotion to director, so I'm moving forward with optimism. In the meantime, I have a lot to offer in my current role and will continue to give it my all. I hope it's OK if I call on you once again in the future as a reference. Thank you so much.

Alex

From:	Rachel Simon
To:	Alex Klein
Subject:	RE: Job interview

Alex, thanks so much for letting me know. I'm sure you feel discouraged and disappointed, but your time will come. You're a star and stars always rise to the top. I have confidence in you! Of course, you may call on me in the future – I am happy to serve as a reference any time. Keep your chin up!

Rachel

I appreciated how forthcoming and honest Alex was, as telling others about our failures is not exactly easy. I'd like to think my encouraging response provided him some comfort and a boost of confidence that his future remains bright.

Sometimes it's impossible to tell who the hiring manager is, as that info might not be included in the job posting. If you think all is lost on this tip, let me assure you it's not, as you can often conduct some detective work to find out who the hiring manager might be. If you use your inner

Sherlock Holmes skills to pinpoint the department with the opening, you might be able to ask around about which leader has the vacancy.

Even if you don't know who the hiring manager is before the interview, you can always use this tip *after* the meeting, as shown in the following example:

From: Zoe Fila
To: Rachel Simon
Subject: Chief of staff job

Hi Rachel, I'm not sure if you know Henry Arnold or not? I had the chance to interview with him today to be his chief of staff. I thought the interview was fantastic and we had an easy conversation and great rapport right from the start. I really want this job!!! I know I could be amazing in it if given the chance.

Would you be willing to send Henry a note on my behalf? He said he's interviewing a few more people and so a note from you may earn me extra consideration. Of course, I sent him a thank you note as soon as I got back to my desk. ☺

From: Rachel Simon
To: Zoe Fila
Subject: RE: Chief of staff job

Done! I just sent Henry a note raving about your many awesome qualities. My fingers are crossed for you! Keep me posted.

Rachel

It would have been great to have a reference before the interview, but in this case it came after. I was more than happy to provide it at any point in time and believe it made a difference with her chances, as Zoe got the job.

I haven't provided a real-life example to illustrate a time when I've personally used this tip. That's because I've consistently been tapped on the shoulder for positions and didn't need to ask my network for recommendations—or so I thought. It turns out, there have been several occasions when my network's endorsement played an integral part in securing a role, without my knowledge. The most significant time occurred when I was promoted to be a vice president. The hiring manager, Mike, was positive he wanted to select me for the role based on our previous working relationship, as he had promoted me once before. Yet his supervisor, John, didn't know me at all and was rightfully skeptical. After the fact, I learned that Mike requested several people of influence to reach out to John to sing my praises, extol my accomplishments, and define my capabilities. All this happened *prior* to me even knowing there was a job opening or that I was being considered. I become emotional when I think about the energy those in my network exerted to ensure I earned the promotion. You'll recall the discussion near the beginning of this book about digging your well before you're thirsty. This is a prime example of that concept, as years of authentic networking led me to that very moment.

I saw this scenario play out once again almost a decade later, when I was asked to take on some new responsibilities in the privacy space. Once I got over my initial anxiety, as I detail in tip 17, I found the work to be energizing and exciting. There was just one problem—it was the perfect work for me but was housed in the wrong department of my large company. The good news is that I knew and admired the chief privacy officer. We had worked together years before, and we had kept in touch via lunches and warm exchanges. I pitched the idea of my team aligning under his at the exact same time that he was reaching the same conclusion that our teams would be stronger together. Tom worked tirelessly behind the scenes to ensure that the move happened—the synergies not only benefitted our company, customers, and team members but benefitted my career tremendously. Would Tom have gone out on a limb to sell the idea to his supervisor, David, and seek the myriad of approvals had we not had a previous relationship? Perhaps. I'll never know. But the fact that he knew my capabilities and positive attitude and that we were already in one another's network could have only helped to secure the new position. Current Rachel owes a debt of gratitude to Past Rachel for the work she did to nurture this relationship that resulted in an amazing, fulfilling job opportunity.

A final anecdote ties these last two stories together. Through hard work, extra projects, and authentic networking, I built a strong relationship with John during my time in finance. The week before he retired, we met for a virtual coffee, and I shared my excitement about my new role in privacy. As soon as we ended our call, John quickly ventured a few offices down to visit his peer, where he proceeded to tell David how fortunate he was to have me in his organization and the positive impact I was sure to make. Wow. I already had the job, but these unsolicited comments served to expedite the trust David had in me. I learned so much from this extraordinarily kind gesture and now ensure I do this for others when they take a new job. What leader wouldn't want to hear from a respected peer that they made a wise hiring decision?

A strong network is valuable for so many reasons, and there's nothing wrong if one of those reasons is to benefit your career. Authentic networking is all about planting and nurturing the seeds of a reciprocal network and enjoying the blossoms of success.

READY TO TRY?

Are you ready to give this tip a try? Here are some sample emails to get your creative juices flowing. Edit them to fit your own writing style and unique situation.

From: You!
To: Antonietta Salvador
Subject: Letter of recommendation?

Hi Antonietta,
I hope all is well! I have applied for a position working for Jasmine in Tech Dev. I believe you have a really good relationship with her from the time she used to work in operations. Would you mind putting in a good word for me?

What makes me a perfect fit for the new role? I have quite a bit of coding experience, know three different programming languages, and have a solid background in technical writing. I am also a strong communicator and people seem to enjoy working with me – at least you did! ☺

I have also attached my resume for your perusal. Thank you so much for the consideration!

You

From: You!
To: Glen Sheller
Subject: Opening on your team

Hi Glen,
It's not a secret how much I enjoyed working in your organization in my last role! Hands down, you have been my favorite vice president during my entire career. I learned so much by observing your leadership style and how you approach problems.

I understand that you have an open position on your current team. Although I love my job right now and feel as though I am contributing at a high level of performance, I would never forgive myself if I didn't throw my hat into the ring for the chance to work under your leadership once again. I believe that Vera is the hiring manager – would you mind letting her know about my skills and what I bring to the table? In particular, I think she would find the work I did on the conversion project to be impressive. If you were to lay the seeds, I could expand further in an interview.

Thank you so much – I also attached a copy of my resume.
You

From: You!
To: Boris Petrov
Subject: Vacancy on Susanna's team

Hello Boris,
Although I enjoy my current job, I'm thinking about a change since I've been in this role for over three years. I heard your peer, Susanna, has a vacancy on her team which I believe I'm perfect for. Would you mind letting her know I've applied? A few traits you've observed are that I'm a:
- Solid performer with a Far Exceeds rating
- Volunteer committee member for employee engagement
- Natural leader who turned around the results of my current team

I appreciate you very much and the time you've poured into my development. I attached a copy of my resume. Thank you!

From: You!
To: Joanna Kleever
Subject: Opportunity with the strategic planning team

Hello Joanna,
I really enjoyed getting the chance to work with you on the strategic planning design process several months ago. I see one of the positions we advocated for has just opened up. Even though the role doesn't report directly to you, I believe you can speak to the vision for the job as we originally outlined and hopefully why I would be an excellent fit. I'm excited about the chance to interview for this role.

Can I please ask you to write a letter of recommendation for me? I have also attached my resume. Thank you!

From: You!
To: Giselle Yanksy
Subject: Possibility of a job change?

Hi Giselle,
It was great to see you at our annual division meeting!

I'm ready for a new challenge to grow beyond my current role. As much as I enjoy working in sales, I'm looking for my next opportunity.

I really look up to you as someone who has a good sense of what our company's future holds. I'm hoping I can schedule a few minutes to discuss how best to position myself for opportunities when they become available. Are you OK if I schedule 30 minutes either in person or virtually?

QUESTIONS TO HELP YOU GET STARTED

- When you apply for a new position, do you know someone who has a relationship with the hiring manager? Can you request a letter of recommendation?

- How will you select the person in your network to ask for a recommendation? Depending on the opportunity, should it be your current supervisor, a mentor, or the highest-ranking person you know? Which would resonate the most with the hiring manager to improve your chances?

- When should the letter of recommendation be sent to obtain the maximum effect? For instance, would it be good to have it sent to help you secure an interview during the initial screening process? Or would it be better to reinforce your skills after an interview?

- Who do you need to close the loop with one way or another to let them how their recommendation went? Have you thanked them appropriately?
- When you ask for a letter of recommendation, what skills and traits will you outline to help tell your story? Be sure to make it as easy as possible for the writer to speak on your behalf.
- Who knows your skills and capabilities and is willing to recommend you to others? If the list is slim, this is an excellent place to add focus before you need the help. A robust network now may help you immensely further down the road.
- Is your résumé in perfect, tip-top shape, ready to go at a moment's notice? Do you have a cover letter template available that you can edit for personalization? Who has reviewed these documents within your network to give you feedback?

TIP 14

Stay Connected with Former Colleagues

You now have an array of ideas to form relationships with countless colleagues, including some you don't know well and others who are "casual strangers." Are you ready for the lowest-risk, easiest tip of all? Reach out to your former colleagues and people you previously worked with. You already know each other, and you have a built-in relationship. Even if it's been a while, it's likely the connection is still there, just waiting to be relit or nurtured.

Just as it's less expensive for companies to retain a customer than to acquire a new one, networking can be viewed the exact same way. Isn't it easier to call upon a former colleague for help, advice, or simply a cup of coffee than to establish a new relationship from the ground floor? There's a need for both, but the former is unquestionably a more comfortable route.

At age twenty-two, I started my career, far from home. The existing management team in my new office had been together for years, some even for decades. They had more years of work experience than I had years alive on the planet! They were a tight-knit group, and I was unsure of how they would accept me as a newcomer. Fortuitously, I hit the jackpot. They were a warm, encouraging team, whereas I was an insecure, unconfident sponge ready to soak up anything that anyone would teach me. They collectively poured all their knowledge into me and rooted for me. They helped me navigate through some tough personnel issues and were proud of me when, in a short period of time, my team rose to the top of the performance leaderboard. Sure, I could tell myself that my success was due to my outstanding management style—who wouldn't want to believe *that* story line—but the truth was these women stacked my team with strong performers who made the road just a bit easier. They invited me over for holidays, introduced me to their families, and savored every detail of my personal life, especially my dating life, that I wanted to share. They were literally the wind beneath my wings—cue the Bette Midler music! When it was time for me to move on from that role to a new lateral assignment across town, our supervisor hosted a going-away party. I read aloud a poem that I had written to thank them for their support. We all cried bittersweet tears and vowed to keep in touch.

And we did! I called on them often for their mentorship and per-spective. When I was promoted, they rejoiced in my victory, and after I moved to another city, we continued to stay connected through phone calls, emails, and holiday cards. Several of these wonderful women traveled eight hours to dance at my wedding.

What a rare gift of unwavering support to receive during my first year of employment. Was I perfect at keeping in touch with these delightful ladies after that? No. We were all busy, we all moved on, and we all focused on relationships with those in close proximity. It happens all the time, even to those with the best of intentions and the strongest of bonds. But later, when I would think of these women, I would send them a note and vice versa, and we would respark our relationships, like the email below:

From: Rachel Simon
To: Tracey White
Subject: Hi!

Hi Tracey,
Hello my friend! It's been a while and you just popped into my mind. How's your job and the whole team? And how is your family? Do you get to see your grandkids often?

We are all good here! Can we catch up soon with a phone call?

Rachel

The notes were always warmly received and reciprocated with equal fondness. More importantly, they taught me that it doesn't matter how much time has passed; it's always great to be remembered and to reestablish a connection.

If I were to challenge you right now to make a list of ten people you could reconnect with, I bet it would be easy. You may not have been the one to move on—perhaps it was them. They may have been peers who switched departments or supervisors who transitioned upon receiving a promotion. Wouldn't it make their day to hear from you?

I do this quite often—when former colleagues pop into my mind, I immediately send a note to reconnect, and I feel delighted when others do the same for me.

In a previous role, I led a team of about fifteen hundred team members. Once I moved on, Mara was one of the few colleagues who maintained a meaningful connection. Every now and then I would receive an email like the one below:

From: Mara Thackerton
To: Rachel Simon
Subject: Hello

Hi Rachel,
How are you and your family doing? I know you're very busy but I wanted to take a minute to catch up with you. I'm doing well given all the changes in my life. My role has expanded to include other functions, which has been very exciting. I once again made the "ready for promotion" list – yay! This gives me opportunities for exposure.

I hope you're doing well. I still appreciate the influence you've had on me. Thanks for everything you did to help me see the big picture.

Mara

From: Rachel Simon
To: Mara Thackerton
Subject: RE: Hello

Hi Mara,
So good to hear from you! Thank you for your kind words – it makes me happy to know that I've had an influence on such an amazing woman! You are easy to support. I'm extremely proud of you and am rooting for your continued success!

Rachel

My connection with Mara is another one that blossomed from a networking relationship into a beautiful mentoring relationship. After this, I encouraged her to schedule time on my calendar for live discussions about her career, motherhood, and life in general. I can trace our close relationship all the way back to our original emails.

This tip is great for reconnecting with colleagues on many levels, but it's also useful when there's a professional issue for which I'd like a fresh perspective. In the email below, I reached out to a former leader I previously worked with to gain his insights.

From: Rachel Simon
To: Percy O'Quinn
Subject: Hi!

Hi Percy,
It's been a while (5 years???) and I hope all is well! You've been on my mind
– not just because I'd like to catch up and hear how you are, but because I
could really use your mentorship.

When you were on our team, you put a lot of effort into transformation and
culture change. I admired your leadership then, but now that I'm tackling
similar issues, I truly appreciate the dynamic and inclusive way you
approached this.

Mind if I schedule 30 minutes for us to catch up and get your thoughts?
Thank you!

Rachel

I was glad I reached out to Percy, and he provided helpful information relevant to charting my new path. Chances are high that there
are colleagues from my past who have encountered just about every
challenging issue I face today, only in a different flavor. It's been such
an easy and effective way for me to tap into their knowledge and mentorship while also making them feel valued that I remembered their
contributions. A win-win proposition!

Another example is from Jamila, a former team member who sent
me this note out of the blue, about two years after she had shifted to
a new role.

From: Jamila Yakowitz
To: Rachel Simon
Subject: Hello

Good afternoon, Rachel.

I just wanted to send a quick note to say hello. I was telling someone yesterday about the mentoring sessions you conducted which I found to be very interesting and meaningful. I always walked away with valuable tips. The ones I refer to the most are the resume and interviewing sessions.

Thanks again for including me in those sessions. I hope all is well!

Jamila

It was wonderful to hear from her. Not only did I appreciate that she thought of me and shared several of the lessons she had learned but it was terrific to reconnect. This prompted me to reply and ask her what she was up to in her role. I noted that she was in compensation within human resources if I ever needed a contact there.

Former supervisors have been prime people with whom to maintain a relationship, since they understand my skill set and capabilities with more clarity than most. Unless I parted ways on difficult terms, which thankfully I never have and hopefully never will, I believe they would appreciate hearing from me and would be delighted to be reminded of how much I enjoyed working for them. That was the spirit in which I sent this note to one of my favorite past supervisors.

From: Rachel Simon
To: Sophie Day
Subject: Hello there!

Hi Sophie,

Someone asked me recently about some of the best supervisors I worked with over my career, and without skipping a beat, I added your name to my very short list. And that made me realize that I hadn't spoken to you in a while and so I wanted to say hi.

Truthfully, you were an amazing boss. You were always direct and supportive and you pushed me to do great things while having my back. I would never have gotten my current job without you.

So what have you been up to? Please let me know how your family is! ☺

Rachel

Sophie responded with gratitude and warmth, and she shared a few photos. Who wouldn't want to receive an email saying they were a favorite colleague, direct report, or supervisor? Of course, only say it if it's genuine and authentic, but it's an easy method to reestablish a connection and make someone's day at the same time. In my opinion, no amount of time could pass that it wouldn't be appropriate to reach out. When you consider it from the receiving end, wouldn't you be happy to hear from a former colleague who let you know you're awesome? *Remember: when done properly, networking makes people feel really good!*

In tip 18, I will recommend sending a note to a colleague when you see a photo that makes you think of that person. I'm not trying to jump too far ahead—stay with me!—but the concept can easily apply to this tip as well. A few years ago, I found a picture that brought back memories of a cherished colleague with whom I had lost touch. I sent her the following email with the scanned-in attachment:

From: Rachel Simon
To: Monica Haverty
Subject: Look at this photo!

Monica!

I was looking for a particular photo of my sisters and I stumbled across this picture of us. It sure was a long time ago! This brings back so many happy memories. Anyway, I'd love to catch up since it's been way way way too long. I'll look for some time on our calendars to connect. Looking forward to hearing about your family and your job!

Rachel

Monica was thrilled to receive my note. She responded immediately, and we set up a meeting the following week. Looking at the photo, we had a lot of laughs about our fashion sense—thank goodness nineties big hair and shoulder pads didn't last for too long!

READY TO TRY?

Are you ready to give this tip a try? Here are some sample emails to get your creative juices flowing. Edit them to fit your own writing style and unique situation.

From: You!
To: Khari Moore
Subject: Hello there!

Hi Khari, it's been a minute! You just popped into my head and I thought I would send you a note to check in. I have such fond memories of the time we spent working together on the merger project – we sure did have a lot of laughs in the process! ☺

I've moved on to a new job as well working in business planning. It's a challenge and I enjoy it a lot.

I would love to hear what you are doing these days. I miss working closely with you! OK if I schedule a virtual coffee for us?

From: You!
To: Sydney Leon
Subject: Moving to your neck of the woods

Hi Sydney,
I just accepted a new job with the company in Miami, which I'm very excited about. I thought I remembered (correctly!) that you had moved to Miami. I hope you're enjoying it.

I'm flying down to look for a house – would you mind if we have a call before I come so I can get your thoughts about areas of town to live, schools, etc.?

Thank you so much – it will be great to reconnect! I loved the time we spent working together in marketing and can't wait to catch up.

From: You!
To: Christina Pock
Subject: Hello there!

Hi Christina,
I can't believe it's been ten years since we last worked together! Where does the time go? I was thinking about when we worked on the new product – we were learning as we went along, and I'm proud of what we accomplished.

OK to schedule some time to chat? I'd like to hear what you're up to and reconnect. Thanks!

From: You!
To: Sundeep Kumar
Subject: Team photo – happy memories!

Hi Sundeep,
I found this photo on my phone from a few years ago – it was taken at the conference when our team won the award for best collaboration. That was a great day!

This photo made me smile and think of you – how about some coffee to catch up? Looking forward to hearing what you've been up to!

From: You!
To: Randolf Berringer
Subject: It's been awhile!

Hi there Randolf!
I just celebrated my seven year service anniversary with the company and was reflecting on the people who have helped shape me. You were my very first supervisor, and to this day, you've had the most influence on me. I thank you for all you did to coach me and help me learn – you made an impact!

I see your title shows you're in advertising. What are your responsibilities? I'd love to catch up and hear what you're up to!

You

QUESTIONS TO HELP YOU GET STARTED

- Who has meant a lot to you in your previous roles? Who should you reach out to? Think about supervisors, direct reports, colleagues, and mentors.
- Has it been a while since you've been in contact? Should you mention the last time you were in touch to jog their memory?
- What do you want to say to them? Should you keep it brief or provide a full update of what you have been up to since you've last been in touch? Would it be appropriate to add a photo or two of your family or a recent vacation? Know your audience on this one.
- Would it be a natural opportunity to reconnect with a colleague during the holidays? How about a birthday greeting? Refer to tip 6 for more ideas.
- When a colleague moves on to a new role, should you mark a date on your calendar to intentionally reach out a few months in the future? What would be the ideal time to check in and reconnect?
- Did something occur in your day that reminded you of a former coworker, such as a funny story or a lesson learned the hard way? Is this a good opportunity to reach out?
- Do you have a team photo you could send to a past colleague to reflect upon the time you spent working together?
- Is there someone who has retired or moved on from your company you may want to reach out to for advice, mentorship or friendship? If you didn't save their contact information, could you find them with an internet search or on LinkedIn?

TIP 15

Be Prepared to Network in a Large-Group Setting

In my introduction, I confessed my networking shortcomings and why one-on-one meetings are infinitely better for my personality type. It's hard for me to walk into a large room of people, even if I'm guaranteed to know someone there. It's even scarier to approach people I don't know. It makes my palms sweaty to think about how disastrous the event could possibly go. I've told myself countless ludicrous stories of how I don't fit in, even when I surely do, and how I don't belong—even when I'm a keynote speaker or panelist! Perhaps you do this as well.

Why is it that some people, like me, despise a large-group setting? After all, how hard can it be? What's the worst that could possibly happen? It's not as if a networking event is a life-or-death situation, and I often jokingly tell myself *I've never lost a patient!* before bravely walking into a room. So why so much fear and insecurity? For me, it comes down to this: I have the impression that everyone in the room knows each other already, and I'm the odd one out. When I walk into a room—whether it's filled with tens, hundreds, or thousands of people—a quick scan convinces me that everyone seems to already be paired up. *Everyone* looks to be talking and laughing comfortably with one another. They all give the impression they're having

205

the time of their lives and enjoying the stimulating conversation. It makes me want to turn on my heels and skip the event altogether, and in the early years of my career I did exactly that. It wasn't until later in my career that I realized the importance of these events and forced myself to go.

As I've peeled back the layers of networking, I've discovered what I thought was reality of everyone enjoying themselves is often a facade. In fact, if participants displayed visible thought bubbles over their heads, I believe they would look something like this:

- "Oh, thank goodness I found someone I know. I'll stick with him so I don't have to meet anyone new."
- "I just met this person. Yikes, it's hard to keep the conversation going."
- "I have nothing in common with her. This is a painful chat."
- "Help! Somebody, please save me from this conversation!"
- "Is he even interested in what I'm talking about?"
- "Can I carry on a conversation with her while still glancing around the room to find someone I know?"
- "Oh, are those snacks in the corner? I'm going to get some."
- And undoubtedly there are people in the room whose thought bubbles would say, "This is an amazing event! I've met some intelligent, kind people and can't wait to follow up." If that's you, well done! Please carry on.

I've concluded that people aren't nearly as comfortable in this environment as they seem. To further the hypothesis, I've conducted my own non-scientific analysis on this subject. It's hardly a statistical masterpiece, yet it's revealing nonetheless. I've asked thousands of people this basic question: "Do you enjoy large-group networking events?" The answer is consistent in that only about twenty percent—maximum—of my colleagues say they do. I've asked this question to coworkers of all ages, backgrounds, levels, years of experience, and type of work they do. Not surprisingly, the percentage increases when I alter the question: "Do you find value in large-group networking events?" As we previously discussed, introverts and extroverts alike understand their importance, which is why they even bother to attend and why companies put effort into their production. Employees recognize that relationships are critical and necessary in the workplace.

I take an amazing amount of comfort in the fact that I'm not alone. If only twenty percent of my colleagues enjoy large networking events and look forward to them, that means *eighty percent* of my colleagues feel the same way I do. What a joyous paradigm shift! Eighty percent of my colleagues hope that someone will approach them to say hello because they have no one to talk to. Eighty percent of my colleagues are waiting for someone to engage them in a conversation. Eighty percent of my colleagues want to form connections; otherwise, they wouldn't have shown up at all. Eighty percent of my colleagues are nervous to be in that room, just like me. Whoa! Before anyone pokes holes in my unscientific study—I'm looking at you, my smart PhD husband!—even if I'm only half-right with my analysis, it still demonstrates that there are plenty of people in the room who are as anxious and overwhelmed to be there as I am.

Please join me in exhaling a massive sigh of relief at this revelation. With this paradigm shift in mind, let's proceed with eight practical pieces of advice for how I effectively manage these events to balance my introverted nature and anxiety with my genuine desire to form new connections.

1. I assign myself a minimum time limit I need to stay at an event. If I'm miserable after, say, fifteen minutes, I'll give myself permission to leave, but I must stay for at least that duration. Sometimes I find myself watching the clock tick by, while other times it's no problem. Knowing I cannot walk in and walk right out encourages me to embrace the spirit of the event.

2. I feel discouraged when I don't connect with anyone after several attempts. So, if this happens, I often take a short break and step to the side of the room to respond to an email or pretend like I have an important text to answer. Yup, I'm not ashamed to say I do that. While it's tempting to leave the room, I stay—just off to the side— which allows me to catch my breath, regroup, look around, survey the landscape, and decide with whom I plan to speak with next.

3. I pay attention to body language. I have difficulty approaching people who are standing up, but for some reason they seem far less threatening when they're seated. It's odd, I know, as it's the same person, just a different posture. It's somehow more comfortable to walk up to a table of people and ask, "May I join you?" or, "Is this seat taken?" than a group of people who are standing. Also, when I'm standing, I try to assemble in a horseshoe shape rather than a circle. It's challenging for a newcomer to join a closed circle; however, if it's a horseshoe shape with an opening, it's much easier for others to join. A friend told me that he watches people's feet. If their feet are pointed directly toward each other, that means they're engaged in a conversation, and it's best not to interrupt them. But if their feet are pointed at angles away from each other, that signals it's a casual conversation, and anyone is welcome to join. I've observed this to be true and find it fascinating. If possible, I avoid people who have their arms crossed or scowls on their faces—they may be the loveliest people in the world, but if options are available, I at least try to find people who *appear* friendly. This also serves as a reminder to watch my own body language so that I don't seem off-putting to others. For instance, even if I'm cold, I try not to cross my arms, as that can make me look standoffish.

4. I join a food or drink line, as I'm more relaxed striking up a conversation with someone in a line than walking up to a random person in the room. I might be the only person in the world who actually

seeks out a line in this situation! It gives me the opportunity to say to the person next to me, "What a great event!"; "Is this your first time here?"; or "How are you affiliated with this organization?" Then I say, "I'm Rachel, by the way," and let the conversation continue from there. If given a choice, I'd rather talk with the person behind me than in front. It can be awkward if we're in the middle of a conversation, and the person ahead cuts it off to order his drink and then moves along, leaving me stranded. But if I'm the person in front, I can still order my drink and carry on the conversation with my body pivoted to talk to both the person behind me and the bartender. If it's a dialogue I'd like to continue, I'll wait for the other person to order so we can remain chatting with drinks in hand. This tip also applies to striking up a conversation in a line for registration, name tags, a photo booth, a swag giveaway table, etc. As I said, I might be the only person on the planet who seeks out a line, but it's an effective way to chat with someone new.

5.   I give myself the goal to connect with just one new person. If I tell myself I need to connect with fifty new people, it's not going to happen. But one person? I can do that. I may need to chat with *five* people to find that *one* connection—unless I strike gold during my first conversation—but it's not an unattainable goal. Then I'll employ all the tools I have in my toolbox. For instance, I'll later send a note to let her know how much I enjoyed our talk and ask to grab lunch or a virtual coffee one day. I'll also often follow up with a LinkedIn invitation to connect.

6.   I am not the best at remembering names, so when I meet someone with whom I want to follow up, I'll make a note on my phone right away when the conversation is over. Sometimes I'll be so transparent to say, "I'm terrible at remembering names. Do you mind if I snap a photo of your name tag?" Often this is met with, "I'm terrible with

that too. I'll snap a photo of yours as well." Bonus points for me for inspiring others while I achieve my goals! Many conference organizers include attendee rosters in their apps or conference materials, which make it super easy for me to keep track of new connections. I'll simply take a screenshot of that person's contact information to later jog my memory.

7.   I draw others into the conversation by making introductions whenever I can. If a colleague I know walks by when I'm speaking to someone new, I immediately say, "Do you know DeSean?" and then include him in the conversation. I also freely compliment my colleagues in the presence of others, especially people of influence. I'll say something like, "DeSean manages my budget, and I'd be lost without him. He does an incredible job of keeping me on track." I know I beam from ear to ear when I'm complimented publicly in front of others; therefore I try to do this for colleagues, especially at an event they may feel insecure about attending. *Remember: when done properly, networking makes people feel really good.* And if I'm the one on the receiving end of the compliment, I'll send that person a note later to thank her for making my day.

8.   I encourage myself to relax and try to actually enjoy myself. Several of my most fulfilling relationships in recent years have stemmed from meeting people in this type of environment. I would have missed out had I given up before I even gave them a chance.

What do I talk about at these large-group networking sessions? Admittedly, the conversations aren't as intimate as they would be if conducted over a one-on-one lunch or coffee. They're general and full of wide-reaching questions that anyone can answer without giving too much thought. It's what's known as "small talk" with a back-and-forth conversation. Some people detest small talk, as it can be viewed as fake. But for me, the whole goal of small talk is to have a casual conversation until an interesting topic comes up, or until there's a spark of something we have in common.

I'm told I'm quite good at keeping a conversation going. That's not an accident—it's because I always have at least five small-talk starters in my back pocket at all times. They may include topics such as:

1. The weather. "Wow, the temperature is perfect out there. I'm so happy summer has arrived. What do you think—do you love it or are you already waiting for a change in season?"

2. The speaker or event. "Wasn't that keynote amazing? I could listen to her lecture for hours. She gave me so many interesting things to consider. What did you like about her speech?"

3. Sports. "How 'bout them Cowboys? Who do you root for?" Yes, even I, a non-sports enthusiast, like to cheer for the home team. I'll admit sports are a dangerous topic for me because my knowledge is limited, and my interest is even more limited! While it's unlikely I'll actually use this conversation starter in a real setting, it's worth adding here because it may be helpful to you.

4. The food. "Have you tried these little desserts? They're incredible. What's your favorite type of sweet?" Chocolate is definitely a topic I'm more likely to initiate in a real setting!

5. Upcoming holidays. "What are your plans for Thanksgiving? Will you stay in town or travel?"

Of course, I'll also typically ask, "What's new in your world?" and "What are you working on right now?"

What do all these conversation starters have in common? They all contain an *open-ended question* that encourages a response and dialogue rather than a simple yes or no.

Once I get past the opening question, I look for an anchor, or something I have in common with another person such as a school, a mutual friend, a love of traveling, etc. The quicker I can find an anchor of a shared interest, the more comfortable I am. "Oh, you lived in California? I was raised there and lived in the state half of my life. What part are you from?"; or "You've recently traveled to Costa Rica? I've been there, and it was fantastic. When did you go?" I follow up with questions such as "What was that like?" and "What did you enjoy most about that experience?" Sometimes I have to dig really deep to find something we have in common, such as, "You breathe? I breathe! Yay!" That's a joke, but I'm sure you know the desperate feeling of searching for a conversation catalyst.

I also have my elevator speech in mind because I need to be prepared to answer the question "What do you do?" which I've learned is a favorite go-to topic for many people at a large networking event. An elevator speech is a blurb that sums up "the professional you" and can be done quickly—for example, the time it would take two people to share an elevator ride. It needs to be crisp, concise, and take no more than thirty seconds. Often I listen to someone talk for twenty minutes and still have no idea what they do for the company! Here is something along the lines of what I say: "My name is Rachel Simon. I'm a mom of two great kids, and I'm a senior manager in privacy. I have responsibility for privacy program operations, internal communications, training and awareness, risk management, and individual consumer choices. Privacy is a hot topic, so it's very exciting and meaningful work."

Ding, ding, ding—that was twenty seconds. I don't recite those words verbatim, but I do say some variation. In twenty short seconds, my colleagues learned what I do and that I enjoy my job. It's important to me to mention I'm a mom. Some people wouldn't add that part, but I do. Remember to always be authentic to who you are.

I listen to the other person's answer of what they do for the company and then make conversation, such as, "Do you work with Georgina in accounting?" or "Are you working on the new product launch?" I find ways to ask questions to learn more and form a connection.

If I receive one-word answers or sparse dialogue in return, I know it's time to move on, and I don't take it personally. Not everyone enjoys small talk. They aren't necessarily cold or evasive people; it just takes practice, so make sure you're the one who practices.

When the conversation's over, whether it was a fruitful dialogue worthy of a follow-up or a quick no-connection chat, I look to make a graceful exit. I'll say something like, "It was great to meet you. I'm going to grab a glass of water," or simply, "It was so lovely to chat with you. Have a great rest of your day." Sometimes I'll even be honest and say, "It was terrific catching up. I've challenged myself to chat with five new colleagues today, so I'm going to get my nerve up to do that." This is often met with a comment of, "Good for you. I should do that as well." More bonus points for me for inspiring others while I pursue my own objectives! Don't overthink your exit. I promise no one will even remember it in this type of situation.

If the thought of attending a large networking session with hundreds of people is inconceivable, start smaller. For instance, a workspace where I was located had a once-a-month event to recognize birthdays and anniversaries. Free chocolate cake and popcorn were enough to lure me into participating, but not everyone attended. While I wasn't surprised at the low attendance, because the floor was full of finance introverts, my colleagues missed out on a low-risk, low-time-commitment opportunity to build face-to-face connections. It was a simple way to ease into networking in a large-group setting. Did I love these events? Nope, not even a little bit. Did I attend? Yes, every single one that I could. Did I mention free chocolate cake and popcorn were always served?

Also, don't underestimate the significance of showing up for your colleagues at events, even when you're feeling shy or not quite into it. Do your best to attend wedding showers, baby showers, retirement parties, and promotion celebrations. These types of milestone events are important to the person being recognized and are also a great way to network and build relationships in a nonthreatening environment.

There you have it: my large-group networking survival guide. It's possible to not only survive the event but also thrive. I've discovered with age and wisdom that few things in life are neither all good nor all bad—life just doesn't work that way. It's possible for a large-group setting to be both scary *and* fulfilling, to be both daunting *and* inspirational, to be both intimidating *and* a moment to be proud of when I not only get through it but even enjoy it.

READY TO TRY?

I don't have any email illustrations in this chapter, since it's based on face-to-face interaction, but I've provided you with many pieces of advice on how to make these events less painful. You are more than ready to try a large-group setting!

QUESTIONS TO HELP YOU GET STARTED

- What large-group networking events are available to you at work? Is there a speaker event or group activity to attend?
- Do you have an opportunity to attend conferences or training sessions where you could employ these skills?

- What goals should you give yourself before you attend? For instance, how long should you stay, or how many connections should you make?
- Have you thought of small-talk questions to ask? Have you considered how you would answer each of those questions in a dialogue?
- Have you considered attending a large-group networking event with someone you know, but setting expectations on the front end that your goal is to branch out and meet new people?
- Once you walk in, do you need to review the layout of the room? The periphery may be a good place to start to survey the landscape and then move inward as you grow more confident.
- Should you make a plan to approach people who are sitting rather than standing or vice versa?
- Have you practiced your elevator speech so that you can deliver it in less than thirty seconds? Does it roll off your tongue easily in an engaging manner?
- How will you eat and/or drink strategically so that you can participate in a conversation without your hands and mouth being full?
- How will you remember colleagues' names so that you can follow up later? What tactics will you employ to reconnect after the event?

TIP 16

Welcome Newcomers

When I joined my company, we operated in only five contiguous states right smack in the middle of the country. Open to relocation, I spent the first few years of my career moving between Kansas and Texas. In each role, I learned an extraordinary amount and advanced my career. To my surprise and delight, we completed a horizontal merger with a similar company that operated in California and Nevada. To my greater surprise and initial astonishment, I was tapped on the shoulder to interview for a promotion in the Bay Area. I was recommended by someone in my network, but soon after I accepted the position I honestly didn't know whether I should thank him or vow to never speak to him again.

Allow me to describe what I discovered the very first week of my new job. My predecessor had resigned under duress, and I never had a single transition meeting with him. My top employee decided to quit the week after I arrived. No one in California even wanted the job, because it was full of dangerous political land mines. That's why my new supervisor, wanting someone fresh from another department within the company, called upon his network to see who was open to relocating for the role. The main takeaway: *ask more questions during the interview*! You may be chuckling right now, but I intend that statement as a serious side tip. I would have taken the job regardless, but the story that unfolded in slow motion before my eyes shouldn't have been such a shock. Oh, and did I mention I was getting married two months later *back in Texas* since my incredibly supportive fiancé—now husband—and I moved right before our nuptials and thus needed to finish our wedding planning from afar?

To make matters worse—yes, it got worse!—I also quickly learned that many of my new colleagues in California viewed my arrival with enormous distrust. After all, the timing was directly after the merger completion, and I moved from Texas, home of corporate headquarters. Was I brought in to fire everyone? Was I brought in to change the culture? Was I brought in to report as a spy? There was even a crazy rumor that women in Texas weren't allowed to wear slacks and could only wear skirts. With pantyhose. Was I brought in to reinforce a new strict dress code? While we were a far cry from the casual jeans culture of today's modern workplace, women were certainly allowed to wear pants, and I had plenty of them.

My confidence should have been at an all-time high, having just been tapped for a big promotion. Instead, it was at an all-time low. I felt overwhelmed and alone. If only I had a friendly colleague to lean on in my new environment.

But there was actually one person with whom I felt the tiniest connection. When an employee takes a new role at my company, an announcement is distributed via email to various organizations. I could hear an imaginary cascading whisper as soon as mine was released, saying: "Who on earth is Rachel?" The silence was deafening, except I received *one* note from a new peer in California acknowledging my new job. Just one. It was quite basic, and I doubt she had any idea how much it would mean to me.

> **From:** Denise Chimely
> **To:** Rachel Simon
> **Subject:** Congratulations!
>
> Rachel,
> I am looking forward to working with you in your new role. Congratulations on your promotion!
> *Denise*

Simple, right? I treasured it. I had one peer in my new organization who at least was open to my arrival. That was a win from my viewpoint. All it took was an unassuming note from one colleague to make me feel more secure. I swiftly sought her out, and she generously provided an insider's view of the organization.

Prior to that humbling experience, I had never thought of sending emails to colleagues upon reading their new role announcements. Since then, I do my best to remember just how important it is to reach out to coworkers when they take on new positions—especially if they're new to the company, especially if they're moving from another city, especially if they're being promoted, especially if they're switching departments, and especially if they're entering unknown territory. In other words, I send words of encouragement in all situations, simply because of how much it meant to me.

As an example, when Ananya's announcement came out that she'd accepted a new position, I sent her this note:

> **From:** Rachel Simon
> **To:** Ananya Bhattacharya
> **Subject:** Congratulations!
>
> Ananya,
> I just heard about your promotion – congratulations! Your past experience will be perfect to add a fresh perspective in your new role. My office is just around the corner from your new boss, so please stop by to say hello!
> *Rachel*

Ananya was delighted to receive my email. I know this because she popped in my office to thank me and chat in person.

When my own vice-president announcement was distributed, I received the email below from Andy, one of the most senior executives in our company. How did I know him, by the way? He was my mentoring circle leader many years ago, and we kept in touch. Please refer to tip 4 on how to build relationships with this type of opportunity.

From: Andy Gleason
To: Rachel Simon
Subject: Congrats!

Congratulations Rachel! This is a great move for you.

Andy

From: Rachel Simon
To: Andy Gleason
Subject: RE: Congrats

Thank you so much! See what a great mentoring circle leader you were – I took all your advice to heart and it got me promoted. Now everyone will want to be in your circle. ☺ I could not be more thrilled and excited.

Thanks for taking the time to write me a note. It means the world to me!

Rachel

From: Andy Gleason
To: Rachel Simon
Subject: RE: Congrats

You did it on your own! Great job and I look forward to seeing what you will accomplish.

Andy

There are two things I'd like to point out about this email exchange: First, I was so pleased to get this note from Andy, as I can imagine how busy someone in his position was, and I didn't even report anywhere within his chain of command. If he could take the time to send a note like this, simply to be thoughtful and boost my confidence, I believe we all can. Second, I want to draw your attention to my writing style—if you know me in person or have ever heard me give a public presentation, you would agree that I write exactly the way I speak. I am an enthusiastic person by nature; therefore I write with exclamation marks and sometimes even smiley faces—you've undoubtedly observed that through the duration of this book. This particular email exchange occurred with a senior officer, and yet I still wrote it exactly the way I would write to anyone else in the company. I urge you to be authentic when you're networking—it's exhausting to try to be someone other than who you innately are!

A few years ago, I had a new boss take the reins of my department, and I sent her the following email to welcome her:

From: Rachel Simon
To: Ava Harrold
Subject: Hi!

Hi Ava,
You have such an amazing reputation and I've been an admirer from afar for a long time – so I'm THRILLED to have the chance to work for you!

I'm happy to bring you up to speed on the work my team manages – in the meantime, I attached a one-page summary of my responsibilities. I'm looking forward to working with you and welcome!

Rachel

Ava thanked me for my kind words, told me that my one-page document was extremely helpful, and shared that she was looking forward to jumping in.

While it's comfortable and easy to send a note to someone you know, this tip works equally well when sending an email to a colleague you don't know as a way to explain your job and how you might interact. Jeni was promoted to a new role in an organization that I supported. I didn't know her, yet I sent her the following email:

From: Rachel Simon
To: Jeni Brady
Subject: Announcement

Hi Jeni, congratulations on your new position! While we've never met, I've heard many terrific things about you. I am in finance and lead the teams for payroll, accounts payable and sales compensation, so if I can ever help you with anything, please don't hesitate to reach out!

Rachel

From: Jeni Brady
To: Rachel Simon
Subject: RE: Announcement

Rachel, thanks so much! What a thoughtful note – I'm sure I'll have all sorts of questions soon so I especially appreciate the offer! Thanks again!

Jeni

I was pleased that Jeni responded so positively to my email. Once we got to know each other, she confessed to having similar insecure emotions to the ones I experience when an announcement is distributed. She wondered what her coworkers would think of her promotion, and if they would feel she was deserving and qualified. My email, from a complete stranger at that point, was the confidence booster she needed to snap out of her imposter's syndrome. *Remember: when done properly, networking makes people feel really good.*

Emails, texts, and social media messages are effortless methods to welcome new members to a team, and as you recall from tip 6, I prefer them because they lend themselves to two-way communication. Resist the urge to simply offer a rushed "congrats" and instead take just a few more seconds to add a personalized comment.

Pause for a moment to reflect on the first day of your current job. Did anyone welcome you and help you transition? If the answer is no, perhaps there are simple ways you can bend the culture, whether you're a supervisor or a peer. Some ideas include: organizing a team huddle or video chat for introductions; hosting a potluck or taking the new employee to lunch; ensuring their work environment is ready to go with equipment and system access; and pairing them with a mentor or buddy for shadowing and guidance. New employees may feel as though they are left to sink or swim on their own—not only can this create anxious feelings but this also can result in poor engagement due to isolation and bitterness that can simply be avoided with a bit of effort. It's not good enough to say, "Well, no one helped me when I got here, and I figured it out on my own."

I would respond, "But don't you wish they would have?"

I've been the recipient of several touching gestures throughout my career. On the first day of my first job, I found a vase of beautiful flowers sitting on my desk as a welcome from my new peers. It was such an incredibly thoughtful token and immediately foretold what a warm team I had joined. Similarly, when I returned to the credit and collections organization after a seven-year hiatus working in other departments, I received a handcrafted tin filled with homemade cookies as a welcome-back gesture from a team member, along with a letter of congratulations. The note was lovely, but oh, the chocolate chip cookies were divine. Do you think I remembered this thoughtful action? You bet I did.

READY TO TRY?

Are you ready to give this tip a try? Here are some sample emails to get your creative juices flowing. Edit them to fit your own writing style and unique situation.

From: You!
To: LaQueesha Banks
Subject: Congratulations!

LaQueesha,
I want to offer my heartfelt congratulations to you on your new role! You are such an impressive leader who focuses on both results AND people. Your new team is so fortunate to have you!

As you know, I lead the business operations team, so if I can ever assist you with anything, please don't hesitate to reach out. Congrats again!

From: You!
To: Louie Bernard
Subject: Welcome to the team

Louie,
I just heard about your new role on the controller's team and I want to be one of the first to welcome you. I've been with the group for two years and I enjoy the team, our leadership, and the work we do. I'm more than happy to give you the lay of the land and offer my perspective if you think that would be helpful.

We will see each other for sure every Monday at the staff meeting. Welcome!

From: You!
To: Deborah Woods
Subject: Congratulations!

Hi Deborah,
I'm looking forward to having your skills and talents on the team. I've already heard from several colleagues who were on the hiring committee that they are ecstatic you accepted the offer to join us.

Once you get your legs underneath you, I'm happy to make myself available to help you with your transition. Welcome!

You

From: You!
To: Carlos Manuel
Subject: Congratulations!

Hello Carlos,
Congratulations on your promotion! I'm excited that you're my new supervisor – I'm looking forward to learning from you and implementing your vision. You have a terrific ability to add value quickly.

My group is comprised of ten analytic professionals. We design predictive analytics to aid decision making, respond to data requests, and collaborate on strategic planning.

If there is anything I can do to help you with your transition, let me know!

From: You!
To: Gabriel Iglesias
Subject: Welcome to the neighborhood!

Hi Gabriel,
We haven't met yet, but I noticed your new nameplate being added to the office next door to mine. I know transitioning to a new role can be a challenge. Considering we are going to be neighbors, I thought I'd reach out to welcome you and make myself available if you have any questions.

Looking forward to having a new face on the floor. Welcome!

From: You!
To: Wilhelm Sawyer
Subject: Welcome to the team (from your work from home peer!)

Hi Wilhelm,
We both have work from home roles in sales. When I joined the company three years ago, I struggled a bit to make initial connections. I wish someone had reached out to me when I first started (aside from my supervisor). In that spirit, I wanted to reach out and say welcome!

I'm happy to connect and share my knowledge. I also have tips on how to leverage our company's technology.

QUESTIONS TO HELP YOU GET STARTED

- Does your company send out announcements when colleagues accept new roles? Or is there another way you learn this information?
- Is there a new colleague you should welcome in a new role? Are you acquainted with this person?
- Is there a new colleague who you are *not* acquainted with who would appreciate a congratulatory note? Can you use it as an opportunity to introduce yourself and your responsibilities?
- Is there someone new joining your department, team, floor, etc., for whom you could be a welcoming light *before* she starts her new role? Don't forget to consider leaders higher in your organization, such as a new supervisor or a new senior leader.
- What can you do to make new employees feel welcome on their first day?

- Does your company have new-hire orientation sessions? Are there opportunities to volunteer your experience to help them seamlessly join the team?
- Could you assist with connecting new members of your team with others in your network? Perhaps a group lunch or video chat would expedite new relationships.
- What is the best medium to convey words of welcome? Is it an email, text, social media app, or handwritten letter?

TIP 17

Use Your Network to Get Your Work Done

You may recall the insecurity I consistently feel when I switch jobs within the company. I wince at the thought of starting over with a new supervisor, department, location, and expectations. New beginnings are energizing, but challenging, especially when I enjoy my current role and don't foresee a change coming down the pike. One time, I even experienced a stealth-like switcheroo when my title, department, and supervisor remained the same, yet my skills and expertise needed to rapidly transition to newly assigned responsibilities. I definitely didn't see that one coming!

Let me detail how that happened. My supervisor asked me to come to her office, where she explained she had been requested to assume some critical program management work related to privacy and data protection. It was far different from the work in our department, and she needed me to quickly pivot to lead the project. As she described the complex assignment, I became more and more overwhelmed by the minute. I hastily took notes and remember thinking that she may as well have just asked me to boil the ocean—*that's* how clueless I was. I didn't even understand the acronyms or words she was using. I felt dazed and confused, and it wouldn't have surprised me one bit if she had asked if I was suddenly feeling ill, as I surely had turned a shade of green. As I headed out of her office, she said, "I don't know anything about this type of work, Rachel, but luckily you do."

Um, no, I didn't. I knew nothing. Zero. Nil. Zilch. You could spell the word *nothing* in a thousand languages, and it would still equate to the extent of my knowledge. I felt like an imposter. Why did she think I could handle this work? It was an important task, with lots of eyeballs on the outcome, and a glaring red deadline for the initial project milestone a mere two months away. I was completely and utterly flabbergasted, and I didn't even know where to start. Yet I didn't tell this to my supervisor. After all, no one appreciates an employee who freezes like a deer in the headlights and needs specific guidance every step of the way. Instead, I smiled, told her that I was excited about the opportunity to work on something different, and thanked her for having confidence in me.

And then I practically passed out in the elevator.

Have you ever had a similar experience? Have you ever been asked to take on a new task in which you had no idea where to begin? Have you ever listened to your supervisor explain a new job and felt like you were underwater because the instructions were so ambiguous and unclear? You may have wanted to groan, fret, drown in uncertainty, or wonder if you were being set up to fail. Those were exactly the thoughts that plagued my mind for the remainder of my unproductive day.

That evening, I received a much-needed pep talk from my remarkable husband. He reminded me that I've seen this movie a thousand times before, and in every version I've journeyed from a massive lack of confidence to resounding success. Yes, that's what I needed to hear! I began the next morning with a fresh perspective and an optimistic attitude. Perhaps I wasn't being set up to fail, but instead was being handed the opportunity to learn new skills and lead a rewarding project. Maybe I was being pushed out of my comfort zone, once again, to a place where I would not only accomplish lofty goals but also gain new insights, knowledge, and connections. It was possible that my unique, collaborative leadership style would be helpful in this new role.

With my newfound lens, I knew exactly what to do. I would use my network to learn—one person at a time, one cup of coffee at a time, and one conversation at a time, just as I'd always done.

I asked around for the names of coworkers who had knowledge of this new program, and then I proceeded to reach out individually in an email like the one below:

From: Rachel Simon
To: Nancy Lincoln
Subject: Time to chat later today?

Hi Nancy,
I am assuming responsibility in Jamie's organization for privacy. I heard you are the one to meet with! Can we get together for an education and see how I can quickly get up to speed?

THANK YOU for your help!
Rachel

I sent a similar note to about ten different professionals, and within a few days I had gathered the information I needed to develop a strategy. When I emailed my supervisor the following week to share my plan of action, I listed all the people I had spoken to. Her impressed reply was, "You've been busy!" I'm glad she noticed. Thank goodness for my network, or I would have still been at the starting line wringing my hands.

If I had to summarize the lesson of this story, it's that I used my network to get my work done.

As I described earlier in this book, I consider networking to be full of "six degrees of separation." I might not know someone, but I know someone who knows someone. For example, here is an email I sent several years ago to one of my colleagues asking for assistance:

From: Rachel Simon
To: Dustin Franklin
Subject: Quick question

Hi Dustin, I hope all is well!

If you can't help, I'm hoping you can point me in the right direction. Do you know anyone working on the new branding campaign? I'm looking for a guest speaker for my next all manager call and the team expressed interest in learning more about this.

I thought I'd check to see if you have any leads for me? Thank you so much for the assistance – I appreciate you!

Rachel

I actually don't have a response to display from Dustin. Within five minutes of sending this email, he had not only picked up the phone to tell me who could help me but then conferenced that person on to chat. Within just a few moments, I had a speaker for my all-manager call. I could have spent all day combing through our company directory, searching for job titles of people who may be working on this particular campaign. By using my network, I had my problem solved almost instantaneously.

Likewise, when I was responsible for finding a speaker for a big conference, I sent this email to Michael:

From: Rachel Simon
To: Michael Bleeker
Subject: Invitation to speak at our finance conference

Hi Michael, I hope all is well and that you and your family are doing great!

Finance is having a conference in Dallas on April 2-3 and I'm leading the planning committee. We made a list of speakers we thought would be terrific to learn from and you are at the top of the list!

Is this something you could accommodate in your schedule? We could work with you on a specific time. Thanks for the consideration!

Rachel

From: Michael Bleeker
To: Rachel Simon
Subject: RE: Invitation to speak at our finance conference

Rachel, for you of course!

Michael

Michael's enthusiastic reply made me wish I had asked for something much bigger than just speaking at a conference! It's worth a quick pause to explain how I knew him. In a previous job, about a decade earlier, Michael and I were on the same team, and I kept in touch with him. I'm not sure he would have been so eager and cheerful to do me a favor if we had lost touch. Having my network in place allowed me to go straight to him with my request rather than needing to navigate through his assistant or chief of staff, which may have prolonged the response time and may have convoluted the invitation.

I'm pleased when I can offer the same help to others, and I do it often. It took me mere seconds to answer the email below from Greg, yet it made his job infinitely easier to have a fast response.

From: Greg Grall
To: Rachel Simon
Subject: Contact?

Rachel, I know this isn't your responsibility, but I'm hoping you can assist. Do you know anyone who works in IT? A consultant has a proposal they'd like to run past our company.

Thanks in advance.

Greg

From: Rachel Simon
To: Greg Grall
CC: Homer Jenkins
Subject: RE: Contact?

Hi Greg, you bet. Homer can help – I've copied him to make the connection.

Rachel

Greg was appreciative of the reply, and it was just what he needed to move forward with his work. He told me later that I was the first person that came to mind when he was stuck and that made me happy. I'm glad he thought to use his network to get his work done.

Having a network in place is critical when time is of the essence. When things need to happen in an expeditious manner, it's important to find the right people to help. In the following email to Camila, I needed to act quickly to assemble a team of specialists and I knew I could count on her to be a second set of eyes to identify any gaps.

From: Rachel Simon
To: Camila Rodriguez
Subject: Cross-functional team – need your input

Camila, I need to quickly pull together a cross-functional team to address an emerging trend in the economy. I've attached a list of who I think should be included - who else? I don't want to miss anyone. Thanks for the help!

Rachel

From: Camila Rodriguez
To: Rachel Simon
Subject: RE: Cross-functional team – need your input

Rachel, that's a good list. I would also include Prianka, Kito, and Aidan.

Camila

From: Rachel Simon
To: Camila Rodriguez
Subject: RE: Cross-functional team – need your input

Thanks for the speedy response. Excellent suggestions – we would have had to start all over if I hadn't included Prianka in the first meeting. Thanks so much!

Rachel

Reaching out to Camila was a huge time-saver. Gaining the valuable opinion of someone in my network prevented me from making a costly omission with the initial invitation list.

It has also been beneficial to have a network in place to provide a different perspective on a problem I might be facing. Sometimes, when I have a challenge that shows no signs of improvement, I reach out to a colleague who has experience with the subject, department, or the people, such as the email below:

From: Rachel Simon
To: Belinda Terra
Subject: A few minutes to chat?

Hi Belinda,
I'm currently trying to resolve an issue with your former department. I know you spent many years there and have a lot of credibility with the team. You have such a natural, professional approach to problems... and I'm stuck. ☺

I'm wondering if I could get your thoughts on a roadblock I'm experiencing. Your feedback and perspective may go a long way to closing this gap. Would you be willing to spare a few minutes to chat? Thank you so much!

Rachel

Belinda was glad I reached out and was happy to assist. Complimenting her on her style and approach to problem-solving might have helped. *Remember: when done properly, networking makes people feel really good.*

Next time you're stuck and overwhelmed, give some thought to who can help you. The answer is likely less than six degrees of separation away.

READY TO TRY?

Are you ready to give this tip a try? Here are some sample emails to get your creative juices flowing. Edit them to fit your own writing style and unique situation.

From: You!
To: Chase Humphrey
Subject: Recognition Program

Chase,

I've been asked to develop a new recognition program for our team. I know you have been the recipient of many accolades in the past (because you're awesome) and I think you'd be the perfect person to ask your perspective on what works and what doesn't. As you can imagine, I don't have an unlimited budget, so I'd really like your ideas on how you've felt valued by your supervisors and peers in the past. Do you mind if I set up some time to chat?

From: You!
To: Blanca Hernandez
Subject: Environmental sustainability

Blanca,

My supervisor asked me to take on a special project regarding environmental sustainability. I confess I know very little about this topic, but I'm quite certain you're an expert! Can I schedule some time to pick your brain about the topic? Thanks for the time and guidance!

From: You!
To: Omari Shiff
Subject: Need help with a calculation!

Omari,

Help, I'm stumped! I'm working on some calculations that don't seem to be correct. Rather than stay up all night trying to figure this out, I'm hoping you can spare 15 minutes for me in the morning to assist. I've always admired that you can look at a calculation and immediately know what's wrong – I could really use your help on this as I'm at a loss. Thank you so much!

You

From: You!
To: Lei Ting
Subject: Resume writing – mentoring circle

Lei,
I participate in a mentoring circle and I'm responsible for finding a speaker for an upcoming session on resume writing. I've heard you speak on this topic before and thought you were excellent! In fact, my resume is in great shape all because of you. Would you be willing to come present this topic to this circle? We can be flexible with dates and times. Thank you!

From: You!
To: Mary Beel
Subject: IT upgrade – your perspective is needed

Mary,
I recall you saying that you were tasked with upgrading software a few years ago for our Customer Relations Management toolset. We're now looking to upgrade it once again, but unfortunately none of the original team members are still around. I've been asked to identify business logic that went into the design and I'm hoping you might share with me an oral history that set the initial direction. Can I please set up an hour for us to discuss? Thank you.

From: You!
To: Elroy Thomas
Subject: Time to chat?

Hi Elroy,
I understand from talking with my boss that you successfully initiated a comprehensive methods and procedures process. I want to replicate your approach in my own division. Could you spare a few minutes to discuss how you approached this as well as the pitfalls you encountered? It goes without saying how much I respect your progress in this area and I'm eager for any knowledge you're willing to share. Are you OK if I set up time to discuss?

QUESTIONS TO HELP YOU GET STARTED

- Is there an expert in your company who can provide some knowledge you need? Would a fresh perspective help you gain new insights?
- Is there someone who is connected—even more than you!—who can point you in the right direction for a problem that isn't theirs to solve?
- Is there a subject you know nothing about but need some information? Who can you ask to join you for coffee or lunch to teach you about a new topic?
- If you're asked to secure a speaker for a meeting, who could you ask within your network? Have you seen this individual present before, and you could request a favor?
- Do you know who previously did your job before you who could provide some history on an issue that is a logjam?
- If you're planning a conference or meeting in a different city, can you leverage your network for speakers, logistics, dining recommendations, lodging, etc.?
- Do you need support with a strategy, policy, or law? Who in your network has connections on that side of the business?

TIP 18

Send a Note When You Come Across a Photo, Video, or Article

The number of times an idea has suddenly struck me to pick up a particular book to read at a particular moment, as if I were jolted by a lightning bolt of inspiration, in round numbers is about zero. I genuinely appreciate a solid recommendation. When I go to the library without a specific title in mind, I stop to scan the area located directly inside the door containing "themed selections" of books the librarians have chosen. For instance, if it's approaching President's Day, they'll display presidential biographies or novels set around the White House. If it's summertime, they'll select lazy-day beach books, and so on. I'm sure it makes their hearts happy every time one of those carefully curated books is checked out by a cardholder.

As social media and crowdsourcing have advanced, I even rely on the recommendations of complete strangers when I peruse reviews for blogs, podcasts, videos, articles, etc. I'm a very average consumer with my tastes. If the majority of the population enjoys a particular video that went viral, there's a high likelihood I'll enjoy it as well. If the majority of the population raves about a specific book, odds are high I'll appreciate it too. If the majority of the population finds a product to be the best thing since sliced bread, chances are good that I will be a fan as well. But when I'm seeking something inspirational that speaks to my inner core, a personal recommendation from someone I know—and who knows me—rather than a complete stranger, will resonate higher. That's how I've found the bloggers, authors, and speakers who have invigorated me the most—directly from people I respect and whose opinions I trust. And I'm sure it makes these people feel good when I take them up on their recommendations. I know it makes me feel good when the roles are reversed.

Sometimes I find recommendations by asking leaders I admire for their top picks. For instance, asking about favorite leadership and management books have led me to consume real gems, such as *The Seven Habits of Highly Effective People* by Stephen Covey and *Good to Great* by Jim Collins. These leadership books have stood the test of time and have had an enormous influence on my workplace style and personal life. In turn, I've recommended these books to others.

Other times recommendations find me in the form of an unexpected email from a colleague. And therein lies the basis for this tip, as it's simply delightful to receive a note along the lines of "I saw this and thought of you" or "you were the first person who popped into my mind when I read this, discovered this, and so on and so forth."

As you know, I'm encouraging you to stay connected with colleagues, and I find that email is one of the easiest, fastest, and least-terrifying-for-introverts ways to keep in touch. But all emails are not created equal. A networking email just to send a networking email can fall flat and not achieve the desired outcome. To illustrate, I offer the following example from Len, a colleague I worked with in another department several years ago:

From:	Len Hendricks
To:	Rachel Simon
Subject:	Hello

Hi Rachel, how are you?

Len

From:	Rachel Simon
To:	Len Hendricks
Subject:	RE: Hello

I'm doing well! And you?

Rachel

From:	Len Hendricks
To:	Rachel Simon
Subject:	RE: Hello

I'm doing well, too. Have a great day.

Len

Um, not very memorable or meaningful, is it? It's not that I was annoyed that he thought of me. I'm always delighted to know I popped into someone's head, and that person was inspired to reach out. But this is not effective networking. There's no call to action, and there was certainly nothing about it that encouraged me to engage further. It was probably the most nondescript, bland email I've ever received.

Now let's contrast this with an email I received from Rochelle.

From: Rochelle Jackson
To: Rachel Simon
Subject: TED Talk – Women in Leadership

Rachel,
How are you? I hope all is great with you and your family!
I want to share a video I came across on TED Talks. In the video, the speaker discusses the challenges of women in leadership, living beyond fear, asking for help and the difference in how men and women are viewed in the workplace. You may have already seen the video, but if not, enjoy! I've pasted the link below.

Rochelle

What an effective way to keep in touch! Rochelle saw this TED talk, thought of me, and shared the link so I could watch it. I watched the recommended video and proceeded to read the speaker's book, all based on Rochelle's recommendation. I also made sure to reply with my appreciation and thoughts.

Similarly, I received this email from Kris:

From: Kris Wiley
To: Rachel Simon
Subject: Networking Article

Rachel,
I saw this article and thought of you. Not everyone is a natural networker which is something I can relate to – you exhibit a lot of these qualities and you make it look easy! ☺

I think you'll enjoy the writer's point of view. I attached the article below.

Kris

I read the article and responded to Kris with my comments. It's such a simple and great way to remain connected. Instead of merely sending a note to say hello, sending a note to say, "I saw this and thought of you," is exponentially more effective. I also appreciated the kind words he had to say about my leadership style. *Remember: when done properly, networking makes people feel really good.*

It's important to know your audience. Would they appreciate an unsolicited recommendation? Instead of just sending it out of the blue, you can tie it to a conversation you've already had.

From: Rachel Simon
To: Rita Qually
Subject: Industry consolidation – new viewpoints

Hi Rita,
It was great to see you for lunch last month. Our conversation was very enlightening and I learned a lot from your perspective on industry consolidation. Today I saw this article and it echoed many of the points we discussed, but with a few different viewpoints that I found fascinating. Just thought I'd share. Enjoy!

Rachel

This email to Rita demonstrated that I not only paid attention to our conversation but also thought of her and wanted to send the article along. She was appreciative and replied back with her comments—she even offered a dissenting view of one of the author's points in the article, which gave me new information to consider.

I often use this tip when I see something that makes me smile, laugh, or think of a colleague. For instance, I sent the following email to Kai. He chuckled as much as I did, as the meme was extremely topical at the time.

From: Rachel Simon
To: Kai Lamana
Subject: Conference Call Bingo!

Kai, I saw this and could not stop laughing – enjoy! It brings back so many funny memories of our time leading the daily productivity calls.

I hope all is well with you – what have you been up to? How is your family?

HI, WHO JUST JOINED?	CAN YOU EMAIL THAT TO EVERYONE?	IS ____ ON THE CALL?	UH, ____ YOU'RE STILL SHARING...	HEY, GUYS, I HAVE TO JUMP TO ANOTHER CALL
(SOUND OF SOMEONE TYPING, POSSIBLY WITH A HAMMER)	(LOUD, PAINFUL ECHO/ FEEDBACK)	(CHILD OR ANIMAL NOISES)	HI, CAN YOU HEAR ME?	NO, IT'S STILL LOADING.
NEXT SLIDE, PLEASE.	CAN EVERYONE GO ON MUTE?	I'M SORRY; I WAS ON MUTE	(FOR OVERTALKERS) SORRY, GO AHEAD	HELLO? HELLO?
SO (cuts out) I CAN (unintelligible) BY (cuts out) OK?	SORRY I'M LATE (INSERT LAME EXCUSE.)	I HAVE A HARD STOP AT...	I'M SORRY, YOU CUT OUT THERE.	CAN WE TAKE THIS OFFLINE?
I'LL HAVE TO GET BACK TO YOU.	CAN EVERYONE SEE MY SCREEN?	SORRY, I WAS HAVING CONNECTION ISSUES.	I THINK THERE'S A LAG.	SORRY, I DIDN'T CATCH THAT. CAN YOU REPEAT?

CONFERENCE CALL BINGO

Rachel

I must emphasize that using humor in the workplace can be extremely risky. Everything you say—and especially everything you put in writing—must be appropriate and sensitive to cultural awareness. Moreover, ensure it would not embarrass you, or place your job in jeopardy if made public. If you wonder if a particular meme, image, GIF, or joke is appropriate for the workplace, and you're unsure, *don't use it*. I repeat: *don't use it*.

On the flip side of sending something funny are notes of condolence. I send them to people I know who are hurting, and they tell me it means a lot. After the loss of my beautiful mom, I received this thoughtful email from my colleague, Thomas:

From: Thomas Matthew
To: Rachel Simon
Subject: Thinking of you

Rachel,
I want to express my condolences to you. I know how close you were to your mom and it must hurt to have her gone.

When my mom died, someone sent me this poem which has provided a great deal of comfort. I thought you would gain some comfort from it as well. It's titled "The Ship" by Bishop Brent.

> What is dying
> I am standing on the seashore, a ship sails in the morning breeze and starts for the ocean.
> She is an object of beauty and I stand watching her till at last she fades on the horizon and someone at my side says: "She is gone."
> Gone!
> Where
> Gone from my sight that is all.
> She is just as large in the masts, hull and spars as she was when I saw her, and just as able to bear her load of living freight to its destination.
> The diminished size and total loss of sight is in me, not in her, and just at the moment when someone at my side says,
> "She is gone"
> there are others who are watching her coming, and other voices take up a glad shout:
> "There she comes!"
> and that is dying.

Thomas

It's difficult to put into words how much this email meant to me, how many times I've read that poem, and furthermore, how often I've shared it with others, just as Thomas shared it with me.

There have also been instances throughout my career when events outside the company have deeply affected my colleagues on a personal level. Instead of ignoring these issues in the workplace, I've learned to reach out, show genuine empathy, and actively listen to gain new perspectives. Below is an example of an email I sent individually to several colleagues after the death of George Floyd:

From: Rachel Simon
To: Ken Lowell
Subject: The news...

Ken,
The news is hurting my heart. The videos I've seen of injustice in our country are beyond troubling and I'm committed to being part of the solution.

I've appreciated our open dialogue about these issues in the past and would love to have another conversation to listen and hear your perspective. Do you mind if I set up time for us to talk?

I just wanted you to know that I'm thinking of you and the community.

Rachel

The response from Ken to this particular email was painful and eye-opening to read and furthered my passion for diversity and inclusion. He was touched and felt seen that I had reached out when I saw the news. He generously shared his thoughts and book recommendations. I continuously grow by taking the time to listen to new perspectives, and I've never once regretted reaching out to engage in dialogue.

To close this chapter on a lighter note, at times I send photos to coworkers when I see something that makes me think of them. I sent this email to Iris when I was on vacation:

From: Rachel Simon
To: Iris Theodore
Subject: Saw this and thought of you!

Hi Iris,
I was on vacation last week in California and saw this gorgeous redwood tree that reminded me of you – I attached the photo. You've shared your favorite Nelson Henderson quote: "The true meaning of life is to plant trees, under whose shade you do not expect to sit." When I saw this majestic tree, you were the first person to pop into my head. Thanks for inspiring me to be a better leader and person!

Rachel

Iris loved the image and immediately responded with her appreciation that I had thought of her. I send topical photos at other times too. For example, a colleague worked extremely hard on a new advertising campaign, and when I saw the billboard for the first time, I snapped a photo and texted it to her with a hearty congratulations for a job well done. Another colleague sent me a book recommendation—when I finished it, I took a photo of myself reading the book and thanked her for her excellent recommendation. My colleague, George, and I have a joke about a T. rex. When I visited a museum and saw the T. rex skeleton display, I couldn't resist texting him a photo, and we shared a good laugh.

I have to state a final reminder that the photos, memes, jokes, books, etc. etc. etc., must be appropriate for the workplace—if you have any question at all about the suitability, *please do not send them!*

READY TO TRY?

Are you ready to give this tip a try? Here are some sample emails to get your creative juices flowing. Edit them to fit your own writing style and unique situation.

From: You!
To: Pedro Morales
Subject: Article – the future of currency

Hi Pedro,
I really enjoyed your Town Hall last week and found your comments about the future of currency to be fascinating. I read this interesting article on how cash may become obsolete and thought I'd share it. You are definitely a thought leader in this space and I always learn something new each time I hear you speak. Thanks for your wisdom!

From: You!
To: Zhang Yong Lin
Subject: Diversity and inclusion article

Hi Zhang Yong,
I found an amazing blogger/speaker that I thought you'd like – I attached the link to his website. His message reminds me of our conversation about diversity and inclusion and how one person can make a difference, just like you're doing! I'm so proud to know you and watch you make a difference in the lives of so many people by recording their stories. Kudos to you and keep doing what you're doing.

From: You!
To: Barbara Roth
Subject: Congrats on your results!

Hi Barbara,
I saw that you were highlighted on our quarterly performance call. Congrats on your remarkable results! I would love to pick your brain on how you moved the needle and achieved success in such a short period of time. Congrats again!

From: You!
To: Penelope Harris
Subject: Tapas in Barcelona

Hi Penelope,
Thank you so much for the restaurant recommendations you provided when I visited New York City. The bistro was unbelievable – the pizza was outrageous!

You mentioned in our earlier meeting that you are heading to Barcelona. You absolutely must try the tapas at Ciutat Comtal. I could eat there every night of the week – the seafood is incredible. It's a fun place with an electric atmosphere. You will love it!

From: You!
To: Yelena Mark
Subject: Cute dog photo alert!

Hi Yelena,
I was out for a walk today and I saw this fabulous dog – I attached a photo. I think it's the exact type of dog that you rescued. Isn't she adorable? It made me smile and think of you so I just thought I'd share it!

QUESTIONS TO HELP YOU GET STARTED

- Is there a particular article, book, blog, etc., that makes you think of someone? Would they appreciate it as much as you do? Who should you send the recommendation to, and what should you say?
- Can you tie your note back to a conversation you had, a speech you heard them deliver, or comments you heard them make?
- Would your recipient appreciate it if you summarized the findings of an article instead of just sending along a link?
- What are the outlets for your specific industry to find news, stories, and daily updates? Should you subscribe to a few sources and then pass along relevant links or articles?
- Was a coworker featured in a news story or publicly applauded for his work? Can you congratulate someone on their results?
- Do you have something in common with a colleague that would serve as a platform for sending a nonwork-related email? Examples include restaurant, travel, or hobby recommendations.
- If you find something humorous, would your coworkers enjoy it? Is it appropriate for the workplace? Be sure to assess the risk before you send it.

TIP 19

Make the Most of Special Projects

During a staff meeting in the first year of my career, my supervisor informed us that the company needed one manager from our department to volunteer with Junior Achievement to teach fifth graders once a week at a local school. She was almost apologetic in her request, as she knew how busy everyone was. I couldn't believe my luck. If I hadn't chosen to pursue a business degree, I surely would have pursued a teaching degree. I was enthusiastic to volunteer, but I didn't immediately speak up, because I thought my coworkers would want this opportunity as well, and I didn't want to appear over-eager. Yet much to my surprise, everyone looked from one person to the other in silence, wondering who would grudgingly step forward. I could hardly contain my excitement as my hand shot up, and I announced that I'd be overjoyed to do it. My peers smiled at me in gratitude for accepting this task, and it taught me a valuable lesson about perspective—one person's burden is another's opportunity. In tip 2, I described my observations about people missing ordinary opportunities to network, and I'll add another thought with a quote attributed to Thomas Edison: "Opportunity is missed by most people because it is dressed in overalls and looks like work."

It's fair to say that teaching Junior Achievement was a lot of work, since my job responsibilities didn't dissipate when I left the office to volunteer for a few hours each week. But I loved every minute of it. I adored the school, the students, the fifth-grade teacher, the curriculum, and I found my groove as an educator that was rewarding to both the students and me. Halfway through the engagement, I had an idea: What if I gave all the students in the class my company's products at no charge for one month and had them create mock advertising campaigns? I asked my supervisor for approval, and she said, "Yes, go for it." Then I wondered if I could ask several company leaders to be the judges for the presentations. I asked my supervisor for approval, and she said, "Yes, go for it." And finally, I wondered if I could invite the top three student winners to present their ideas to our vice president. Again, I asked my supervisor for approval, and she said, "Yes, go for it." And so I rolled my plan into action, to much acclaim and success. The students and I were featured in a flattering news article that highlighted the school, Junior Achievement, and my company, and I marveled at my good fortune to have hit gold during my very first year of employment.

There are three key lessons for me in this story: The first is to be a supportive supervisor when I'm in a similar position to let my employees shine. It took minimal effort for my boss to lend her encouragement, yet it meant the world to me. The second is to raise my hand for opportunities, even if it means additional work. Good things often stem from saying yes. And the third is to make the most of special projects. I did indeed take the students to our regional headquarters, and I was proud of the kids for how much determination and creativity they poured into their work. My vice president, Ray, was engaged and entertained by the presentations, which is how I got on his radar and developed a strong relationship that spanned decades. I kept in touch with him throughout the years, using many of the examples I've shared throughout this book, which included thank-you notes, holidays greetings, and emails of congratulations whenever I saw his name on an announcement. He offered me my first promotion to a second-level manager, and when he was one of our most senior officers he tapped me on the shoulder to serve as his chief of staff in Dallas—fourteen years after our initial meeting in Kansas City. Who knew that volunteering to teach Junior Achievement would not only be a wonderful experience to help my local community but that it would also establish a strong network that would benefit my career?

I've kept these lessons in mind as I consistently view extra work as opportunities, not only for gaining exposure and learning new skills but also for networking.

The Employee Giving Campaign is a big deal at my company, which is a time for employees to pledge money from their paychecks to the charities of their choice. The campaign historically entails a tremendous amount of work in a short period and requires strong matrix management of many different departments to come together for a common goal. When I was new to one of my roles, I asked my supervisor how the leader of the finance campaign was selected. He responded that usually there was a meeting of some sort, and whoever walked into the room last had to lead it. He was only half-joking, as I learned that happened more than once! When I told Kevin I would take it on, I felt a bit like Katniss Everdeen from *The Hunger Games*, exclaiming, "I volunteer as tribute!" I knew it would demand a lot of effort at a point when I still had something to prove in my new job.

I was right. The workload was enormous, but I also got to stretch myself to learn and develop innovative fundraising ideas. Looking at it as an opportunity to meet new people and form new relationships, I sent an email like this to every officer in finance:

From: Rachel Simon
To: Larry Clark
Subject: Employee Giving Campaign

Hi Larry,

I'm honored and energized to lead the Employee Giving Campaign for finance this year. I'd like to schedule 15 minutes on your calendar in the next week or so to discuss a few items:

1. Who would you like to represent your team on the committee?
2. Do you have any strong leaders on your team to tap to lead special fundraisers such as t-shirt sales and a food cart extravaganza?
3. What are your best memories from your team's most successful campaign?

Thanks – with your help, I'm looking forward to our best campaign yet!

Rachel

I could have managed these questions solely by email, and in truth, two of the executives didn't have the time—or desire?—to meet in person. But for the rest, it was a terrific way to have a face-to-face meeting, especially with leaders with whom I didn't regularly interact. The third question on my list yielded some great conversations about best practices and pitfalls to avoid and invoked heartfelt memories about the excellent work their teams had done in their communities. This discussion point in particular yielded a connection and set the tone for future interactions. The campaign was the most effective we'd had in recent years, and I believe the human connection with the leadership team is what added the extra element.

As another example, the Women of Finance became a strong employee group immediately after we launched. To ensure everyone knew about the opportunities available, my department's leadership decided we would have an additional focus on engagement. We recruited Teresa to be a liaison, which was a short-term unofficial position designed to stimulate membership. In the email below, I introduced her to Sabrina, the president of Women of Finance:

> From: Rachel Simon
> To: Sabrina Singer
> CC: Teresa Norris
> Subject: Women of Finance Liaison
>
> Hi and happy new year! Kevin has decided to have a Women of Finance liaison for his team. He has the largest team in finance, but we're not sure we are proportionally represented in membership. Teresa Norris, copied on this email, has stepped up and volunteered to take on this role which is terrific. She has a lot of great ideas on how to improve our participation. Thanks!
>
> *Rachel*

It's the type of note I send often to make a connection between two colleagues, so why am I highlighting this as an example? It's because of what Teresa did next. *An entire year later*, after tremendous success, I was happily surprised to receive the following email from her, attached to the original note:

> From: Teresa Norris
> To: Rachel Simon
> Subject: FWD: Women of Finance Liaison
>
> Hi Rachel, happy new year once again! I was looking back on this past year and wanted to thank you for the opportunity you provided me to be the liaison for Kevin's team. We accomplished our goals and the membership from Kevin's team increased with the "each one reach one" campaign.
>
> I look forward to this new year and expect great things for our organization!
>
> *Teresa*

Teresa did a terrific job in her role as our liaison, and she sent me an email to remind me of that fact. I admire the self-confidence she displayed to advocate for herself and earn the applause she deserved. I learned from her, and now when I'm offered a special project, I consistently thank the person who asked me to do it. Yes, you read that right: I thank the person who loaded up my plate with extra work, as I've discovered it's an easy and effective way to network.

For instance, I served as a panelist at a conference for diversity and inclusion. It was a fabulous event that lasted several hours, so it was a significant time commitment. At the end of the day, I sent this email to the coordinator:

From: Rachel Simon
To: Mandy Candon
Subject: Thank you for the opportunity to speak on the diversity panel!

Hi Mandy,
First, congratulations on such a spectacular event on diversity and inclusion! The room was absolutely buzzing with excitement to be able to engage in such a meaningful way on an important topic. The event was warm and genuine, and reflects your core personality. I hope you're walking on air!

Second, I want to thank you for the opportunity to serve as a panelist. It was an honor to be asked to share my experiences mentoring people of all races, religions, and sexual identities. I know there are many leaders you could've asked and I'm touched that I was included. It was an extraordinary day that made me feel proud and hopeful – congrats once again.

Please keep me in mind for future events – I'm happy to help. Thanks!

Rachel

I could jokingly argue with a wink that she should have been the one to thank me for participating, as outlined in tip 12. But since I also prescribe to this particular tip of making the most of special projects, I didn't mind one bit being the one to reach out. Speaking about diversity and inclusion is a passion of mine; therefore it's important for me to have a strong network of people who know to call on me. I congratulated her on a successful event—*remember: when done properly, networking makes people feel really good*—and asked to be kept in mind for future opportunities. Guess what has happened? I've been selected for many speaking engagements on this subject, which brings me enormous joy and fulfillment. Would I have been given future opportunities if I hadn't sent a note? Perhaps I'll truly never know. But I do know that being a gracious, easy-to-work-with colleague has expanded my opportunities, not limited them.

In one of my early roles as a vice president, my team did not have its own internal company website to showcase our team's accomplishments and serve as an information hub for others in the company looking to learn more about our team's responsibilities. I tapped one of my smart, eager team members, Carrie, to design it for us. She was honored to be asked and confessed she didn't know how to build a website but that she would learn. Several months went by, and I didn't hear anything more beyond our original brainstorming meeting. Curious about the status, I clicked the test link and was surprised to find our new website was built—and it was beautiful! It was well laid out, chock-full of helpful information, and I was more than pleased. I called her immediately to express my delight and coached her by saying, "Carrie, be sure to use these types of extra projects to gain exposure. I would have loved for you to schedule time on my calendar to unveil the final product. You could have said, 'Rachel, I didn't know anything about building a website, but here's what I learned; here was my thought process; here is how I approach something new. Thank you for the opportunity to learn and grow.'" She appreciated the coaching and took the advice forward to her next special project.

This tip can be used for something simple, such as attending a meeting as a representative for a colleague. When my boss went on vacation and asked me to be her delegate, I leveraged this one event into two opportunities. First, I sent the following note to my boss upon her return:

From: Rachel Simon
To: April North
Subject: Welcome back!

Hi Boss,
Welcome back from vacation! I can't wait to hear all about your trip. Thanks for the opportunity to sit in as your delegate while you were out. Things were relatively calm and there were no fire drills - phew! ☺

I took thorough notes from the meetings I attended on your behalf - they are attached in a document and I highlighted any actions that you have. There are a few action items that required immediate attention so I got started on those. I've noted the next steps and who is on point.

Thanks again for trusting me to be your delegate – I'm happy to do it anytime!
Rachel

April was pleased to return from vacation to my timely, organized rundown of the important meetings she missed. She also noted my enthusiasm for serving as her delegate, and I was asked to serve in this capacity from that moment on. While others on her team had previously groaned to be asked to attend extra meetings in her absence—remember the aforementioned Thomas Edison quote about opportunities being disguised as hard work—I viewed this as both an opportunity to be helpful and also to gain exposure to others. I learned a lot while filling in for her and wanted to expand both my knowledge and my contacts. With that in mind, I sent this note to the organizer of one of the meetings I attended:

From: Rachel Simon
To: Conrad Birmingham
Subject: Great meeting!

Hi Conrad,
Great meeting today – I sat in as a delegate for my boss, April North, while she's on vacation. I was not familiar with the work you're doing and you did a really nice job of explaining your project to those who were attending for the first time (like me!) even though the project is mid-stream.

Our paths had not crossed until today and I'm so glad they did. Mind if I schedule a coffee for us to chat a bit more?

Rachel

From: Conrad Birmingham
To: Rachel Simon
Subject: RE: Great meeting!

Hi Rachel, thanks for reaching out. You were value-added to the conversation today – I'm glad you felt comfortable asking questions.

Yes, I'd be happy to get coffee – you can work with Jo to schedule.

Conrad

This was the start of my relationship with Conrad, which can be traced back to this email exchange, and it was so simple to put in motion. I attended the meeting anyway and paid close attention, so why not use it as a chance to network with someone new?

Be on the lookout for extra projects—as we've discussed several times in this book, the opportunities to shine are literally everywhere! And then be sure to take one step further by utilizing those extra projects to expand and strengthen your network. I love the quote by Roger Staubach that says, "There are no traffic jams on the extra mile." So hit the gas pedal and floor it!

READY TO TRY?

Are you ready to give this tip a try? Here are some sample emails to get your creative juices flowing. Edit them to fit your own writing style and unique situation.

From: You!
To: Michelle Greenly
Subject: Internship Program

Hi Michelle,
What a wonderful experience I had supervising our summer interns – thank you so much for the opportunity! I gleaned many new insights, as this was my first time in a supervisory capacity, and I learned that I love leading teams. I know the interns equally enjoyed working with me. They told me that their affinity for the company stemmed from the strong relationships we built. That makes me proud and happy.

Please keep me in mind to lead a team on a more permanent basis if an opening becomes available. Thanks again for this amazing opportunity!
You

From: You!
To: Zane Anderson
Subject: New hire orientation – thank you!

Hello Zane,
Thanks for the opportunity to speak at your recent new-hire orientation. I was delighted to not only share the work that my department does, but also about my personal experience in the company.

The orientation was extremely well managed and put together – I can tell how much time and effort went into all the small details to make it flow so smoothly. Well done!

I'd be more than happy to help at any future orientations – just let me know!
You

From: You!
To: Roman Boinaro
Subject: New reports

Hello Roman,
Thanks for the opportunity to revamp our reports. I appreciate you trusting
me with your vision to give them a fresh and modern feel. My knowledge was
limited in this area when you assigned this special project to me and I'm
proud of what I've learned about coding and design.

Are you OK if I schedule time with you to review the new reports and show
you the layout before we go live? Thanks for the opportunity – it's been a
great experience!

From: You!
To: Cynthia Relita
Subject: Heart Walk

Hi Cynthia,
I'm leading the Heart Walk this year for our organization. You're a hard act to
follow because you did such an amazing job last year! Can I schedule a few
minutes to chat to understand all you did to manage such a successful
campaign? Thanks so much!

From: You!
To: Mason Baird
Subject: Opportunity to present?

Hi Mason,
Once again, thanks for trusting me with the strategic vision for our product
roll out. You'll be pleased with the fresh ideas the team has developed. Would
you please advocate for us to present to our senior leadership prior to the
launch? It would be good for them to be informed of where we are headed,
as well as provide the team some exposure for their hard work. Thoughts?

From: You!
To: Felix Lewis
Subject: Job Shadow – Thank You!

Hello Felix,
Thanks for allowing me to shadow you as you coordinated the customer focus groups over the last two weeks. I'm excited to see the final results of the study. I'm surprised at how much I enjoyed the process of hearing directly from our customers. This would not have been possible without you graciously allowing me to follow you and learn from a pro. You're not only knowledgeable but effective at what you do.

Thanks again for the opportunity and please keep me in mind should an opening on your team become available. Thanks!

QUESTIONS TO HELP YOU GET STARTED

- What are some special projects you should consider volunteering for that might give you additional exposure? Think about fundraisers, employee events, community service, and more.
- How can you use those opportunities to knock it out of the park while you learn new skills and meet new people?
- How can you leverage the opportunities to build relationships? What advice can you seek from others who have engaged in a similar project before you?
- How can you seize a moment when your colleagues are reluctant to volunteer? Is this a signal that it's an excellent opportunity to stand out?
- How will you manage your time to ensure success? Remember that volunteering is one thing, while succeeding is another. Be sure only

to accept a special project if you can devote the time to be successful without your primary role suffering.

- How can you be in tune with company priorities, which may yield special projects? Be alert to articles, newsletters, social media postings, etc., that may give you clues about additional opportunities to shine.

- How should you frame a conversation with your supervisor to enlist support for taking on more work if you have the bandwidth? How can you provide assurances that your "day job" won't suffer from an additional workload?

TIP 20

Let Colleagues Know You're Leaving and Make a Plan to Keep in Touch

've always admired people who knew exactly what they wanted to be when they grew up. As a child, I wanted to be an elementary school teacher, until new interests emerged. I had a short spell of a desire to be a doctor—that is, until I witnessed open-heart surgery and barely lasted two minutes in the operating room before I nearly fainted. Clearly, practicing medicine wasn't destined to be my career choice. But predominantly, I knew I wanted to work in an office. At the young age of about nine, my highest ambition was to manage a doctor's or ortho-dontist's office. I carefully watched the receptionists behind the desk as I entered, secretly wondering how I could perform their jobs better. I felt as though I could efficiently multitask scheduling appointments, managing billing inquiries, and greeting patients—oh, such confidence! I saved my allowance to purchase a plastic "inbox" in which my family would place my outgoing and incoming paper mail, as if I had copious amounts! I still keep that plastic inbox on my desk—a little tattered and a little cracked—as a reminder that I'm living my dream. After all, I do work in an office; I just hadn't dreamed big enough.

Decades later, though I still work in a large office, I have only partially determined what I want to be when I grow up. I excel at leading and managing teams, but I've learned to be open and flexible in which capacity I do it. One of the reasons I was enamored with my big corporation was the ability to pivot my career and try new roles. As a result, I've switched positions within the same company at least sixteen times over the years. In fact, in a pleasant twist, while writing this book, I was asked to change jobs twice from finance to customer care to privacy. When I say that the tips I offer are fresh, relevant, and that I practice what I preach, I absolutely mean it!

One particular time, after I moved past the whole *I don't want to switch jobs* and *I can't do this new position. Why did they choose me*? self-doubt, I was ready to roll. My former team and I had been through a lot during our time together, and I was emotional to depart. I scheduled conversations individually with each of my direct reports, and I sent this note to the members of my extended leadership team, another level down:

From: Rachel Simon
To: Simon Leadership Team
Subject: So long for now!

> By now you've seen the announcement that our finance team will be transitioning to my peer and I'll be moving over to customer care. I'm excited about the new opportunity but will miss working with this fabulous team.
>
> It has truly been a pleasure working with each of you. I am a raving fan of your work and your contributions...and of you as amazing human beings. Please keep in touch!
>
> *Rachel*

The email served as a launchpad for the two-way communication I've written about. My inbox was flooded with replies from team members wishing me well and vowing to remain in contact.

I also sent separate notes to each of the partners with whom I worked closely. I sent these emails one by one, although they had a similar message. I wanted them to hear about the move from me in a prompt fashion.

From: Rachel Simon
To: Craig Spellman
Subject: Announcement

Hi Craig,
An announcement was just released that I'm moving on to a new position within customer care. I've really enjoyed working with you – you're a talented leader with a great vision and keen insights. I know things are hectic right now so I hate to leave in the middle of our big project, but I'm confident my successor will make it seamless. I wish you the best and will keep in touch!
Rachel

The emails had the desired effect. My partners appreciated hearing the announcement from me instead of through the grapevine, and I also received many kind messages in return.

I received this thoughtful email from Dirk when he took a new role in another group:

From: Dirk Bloomington
To: Rachel Simon
Subject: Announcement

Hi Rachel, I've officially accepted a job offer for another business unit, and while I'm very excited, this means I cannot participate in the leadership program you selected me for. I'm still extremely honored to have been chosen for this program and wish you nothing but the best.

Thank you for believing in my potential and I hope I will see you again down the line working for this great company!
Dirk

This email was so lovely to receive. I wonder how many times employees change jobs, and it goes unnoticed. He took the opportunity to inform me while also reminding me that he's a top performer. I sent a note in return to thank him for all he did for our team and let him know that I would miss his bright, optimistic personality.

Likewise, I received the following email from Meghan when she was promoted to a new department:

From: Meghan Wentworth To: Rachel Simon Subject: My Announcement

Hi Rachel,
I wanted to take a moment to thank you for the mentoring and guidance you have given me over the last two years. It's been a joy to work in your organization and I have learned and grown as a result of my time there.

I'm excited for this new, and I'm sure, challenging opportunity. I would love to stay connected and get lunch in the next couple of months to touch base.

Thank you for welcoming me into your organization and helping me flourish!
Meghan

I would have learned of Meghan's advancement through other sources, but it meant a lot that she told me herself since I had been instrumental in hiring her into the company and had been such a strong supporter.

And take a look at the following beautiful email I received from Jessica when she moved on to a new role:

From: Jessica Phelps
To: Rachel Simon
Subject: Thank you!

Rachel, I wanted to let you know that I've accepted an opportunity within human resources. Words are not enough to express my appreciation for you and all you have given me over the years but I'd like to give it a shot...

The first time I heard you speak, I was absolutely inspired by your vision, your values and your attitude toward life and work in general. In that moment, I felt great passion and pride in being a part of your organization.

Since then, I've had the great pleasure of interacting with you both personally and from afar, and can confirm that my feelings on this have never changed. When I try to put a finger on it, it's a drive to make you proud – even knowing that you probably aren't even aware of my day to day work and responsibilities.

Some of the things you've taught me that I'll take with me into my future are:
• Be reflective
• Be a lifelong learner and own it
• Listen
• Bloom where I'm planted
• Network and build relationships
• Find my personal work/life balance

I wanted you to know how much of an impact you've had on my life so far and I hope to stay in touch if that's OK with you.

Jessica

Wow! Jessica's email was definitely a keeper. I was her boss's boss's boss. She didn't have to send me such a thoughtful, heartwarming email letting me know how much she learned from me. *Remember: when done properly, networking makes people feel really good.*

When each of my children was born, I took maternity leave for six months. As my due date approached, I reached out to my partners to share my plans. Of course, I had also worked this out with my supervisor and held face-to-face conversations with each of my direct reports. That way, everyone knew what to expect during my absence.

From: Rachel Simon
To: Vincent Neely
Subject: Maternity leave

Hi Vincent,
As you know, I'm expecting my first child on September 20 – it's getting close! I'm excited to meet this little one – we've decided to be surprised with the gender. ☺

I will be on maternity leave for six months. In my absence, Janeen will be assuming my responsibilities. We've already had several conversations and she is up to speed on the project we're working on. I know she will do a great job while I'm out.

I'll add you to the distribution once I have the baby. Until then, please continue to come to me with issues. Thanks for all your support!

Rachel

My colleagues were thankful for the heads-up on the transition plan, and once again it lent itself to two-way communication and well-wishes. You'll notice I indicated my due date was September 20, and guess what day I delivered my firstborn? September 20. Those who know my organized and efficient personality think it's absolutely hysterical that I gave birth on my actual due date. After all, if I write "have a baby" on the calendar, that's what I needed to do!

This tip works equally well if you're leaving your company to seek other employment. Assuming you're not departing under poor circumstances, your colleagues might want to know where you're headed and congratulate you. As discussed in tip 11, be sure to send the emails individually rather than blind copied for maximum effect. Don't forget to add your contact information and a sincere compliment of how much you've enjoyed your working relationship, such as this one I received from Fiona:

> From: Fiona Sharp
> To: Rachel Simon
> Subject: Last Day 6/1
>
> Rachel,
> I wanted to let you know that I am leaving the company to try my hand at a
> small start-up. It has been an amazing six years here and it's hard to leave
> such incredible colleagues. But I've always wanted to be part of something
> new from the ground floor so I'm going to give it a shot!
>
> I would love to keep in touch. You have my mobile number and my email is
> fiona@keepintouch.com.
>
> You have been an outstanding partner over the years and you have a bright
> future ahead of you. Best of luck!
> *Fiona*

This tip is also an excellent way to let colleagues know when you're
planning to retire from the company. I received the following email from
a key partner in human resources informing me of his departure plans:

> From: David Marquis
> To: Rachel Simon
> Subject: My retirement
>
> Rachel,
> I wanted to let you know that I've elected to retire from the company. I
> decided as part of my retirement, I needed to reach out to some people and
> let them how impactful they are/have been. I think you are an amazing
> leader and person who feels and cares profoundly and deeply about family,
> co-workers and the world. And you don't sit by idly – you take action and I
> admire that about you. The world needs more people like you. If we allow
> ourselves, we learn more from the people we interact with than we could
> ever imagine. Thank you for sharing your story and insights with me.
>
> I've pasted my personal contact info below and am also on social media –
> please keep in touch.
> *David*

What an encouraging email to receive from a respected peer, and his final mentoring gift on his way out provided an extraordinary lesson. I receive plenty of group messages when colleagues retire, but I had never received a thoughtful, personal email like this one. I will undoubtedly send similar personalized notes one day in the future when I retire to those who have impacted me and influenced my career and life.

We spend so many hours at work investing in relationships. It would be a shame to let the connections fall to the wayside every time we switch jobs, whether inside or outside the company, or even when we retire. Each new job opportunity should be looked upon to grow and enhance new relationships, not substitute for the ones that already exist.

READY TO TRY?

Are you ready to give this tip a try? Here are some sample emails to get your creative juices flowing. Edit them to fit your own writing style and unique situation.

From: You!
To: Leeza Huggins
Subject: Moving to a new role

Hi Leeza,
I'm not sure if you've heard the news that I'm moving on to a new role within the engineering department. I will miss working with you! You were the first person I met on my first day with the company five years ago – I will never forget your genuine warmth and encouraging words as you taught me everything you knew. I can't thank you enough for taking me under your wing and guiding me to success.

I'm not going far – just to another floor, so I'll be sure to schedule lunch for us in a few months. Thanks again for everything!

You

From: You!
To: Lenny Ford
Subject: Thank you and let's keep in touch

Hi Lenny,

I've accepted a new position within corporate strategy. My successor hasn't been named yet, but I'll be sure to brief my boss on all of the critical dates and deadlines so that you're not left alone on this big project. There are some milestones coming up and I don't want them to slip.

It has been a pleasure working with you over the past year and I wish you nothing but the best. I admire your can-do personality and sunny sense of humor. Best wishes!

From: You!
To: Oliver Wently
Subject: My retirement

Hello Oliver,

I can't believe the time is finally here – retirement! Next Friday is my final day in the office. The best part of retirement will be spending extra time with my grandchildren. The worst part will be not working with fabulous colleagues like you. I've appreciated every single time we've interacted – you are smart, curious, humble, and gracious. Thank you for the many conversations we've shared. You called them "mentoring sessions," and I agree, because I equally learned a lot from you. I do hope you'll keep in touch and I've pasted my personal contact info below.

You are a shining star and I look forward to your continued success!

From: You!
To: Amrita Laghari
Subject: Many thanks as I move on...

Hi Amrita,
It has been a privilege to serve in your organization for the past five years and I'm excited to tell you I've accepted a promotion in marketing.

You've been the best senior manager I've ever worked for and even though there are three levels of management between us, you've always been so accessible and approachable. My skills and strategic thinking have grown exponentially under your leadership and I will forever be grateful for all I've learned from you.

Thank you for setting me up for success. I promise to keep in touch!

From: You!
To: Chuck Durango
Subject: Upcoming Family Leave

Hello Chuck,
After months of anticipation, our little bundle of joy is here – my partner and I are over the moon!

I wanted to let you know that I'll be taking several months of family leave. I don't have a return date yet, but it will likely be the end of the year. I have briefed my peers on the projects we've been working on together and they've committed to a seamless transition.

Thanks for all of your support and I'll be sure to get back in touch when I return. Good luck with everything!

> **From:** You!
> **To:** Enrique Garza
> **Subject:** Ex-pat assignment in Spain!
>
> Hi Enrique,
> I've been accepted for an ex-pat assignment in Spain. Words cannot describe how excited I am! Our conversations about your experience working overseas inspired me to seek out this opportunity. The thought of being able to work in my family's country of origin – and stay with our great company – is a dream come true.
>
> I'll keep your thoughtful advice in the back of my mind as I transition. Thanks for helping me explore this path and I promise to keep in touch!
>

QUESTIONS TO HELP YOU GET STARTED

- Who should you let know you're moving on to a new position?
- Who within your own department, as well as key strategic partners, should be among the first to know with either an email, phone call, or individual chat?
- Who in your leadership chain do you have a relationship with who you should thank for all you've accomplished and all you've learned from them during your tenure? If you've recently been promoted, who helped to position you for this new opportunity?
- Will you be temporarily leaving for a personal matter, such as family leave? Should you let your peers know of your plan so they don't wonder where you are?
- When you retire, who should you proactively reach out to with words of affirmation and gratitude for your successful career? Who could you make feel good as you leave?

- What thought have you given to helping your successor be effective with a smooth transition? Can you introduce him to the team and key strategic partners?
- How will you plan to keep in touch? Should you make a note on your calendar to schedule lunch with former peers?

AFTERWORD

'll bring us back full circle to the introduction, where I confessed how challenging it used to be for me to participate in large networking events. Each time, I entered the room with high hopes and proportionately high anxiety. Yet each time, I departed without any new meaningful relationships to show for my efforts. For years that was my idea of networking, and I was miserable at it. Happy hours, stacks of business cards, and unproductive chitchat just weren't ideal for my introverted personality. Perhaps you saw yourself in my story.

Once I pivoted to developing authentic relationships and just being myself, my connections increased exponentially. I don't believe it's a coincidence that my fulfillment, friendships, engagement, and career trajectory increased exponentially at the same time. While this wasn't a natural, innate strength, I learned to grow this skill with clear intention and practice—one person at a time, one cup of coffee at a time, and one conversation at a time.

This book aims to share exactly how I accomplished that, with real tactics to demystify the nebulous, frightening concept of networking. I hope you now have a book filled with highlights, notes, underlines, tabs, stars, and arrows—is it only me who marks up books when they're full of ideas I want to implement? I hope you have a list of *practical-for-your-personality* tips that you can apply to a myriad of circumstances. Most importantly, I hope you've discovered the confidence and resolution to start, now that you've gained the perspective that when done properly, networking makes people feel really good.

If all twenty tips didn't speak to you, no problem! Whenever I read a self-help book, I strive to take away just a few worthwhile nuggets to immediately put into action. Surely you got at least a few, right? You now have sample verbiage to send that email, arrange that lunch, schedule that virtual coffee, or reach out to your coworker to say hello. There's no better time to start than today.

Writing this book has been a fascinating—and therapeutic—journey in numerous ways, as I've reflected upon my successes and failures, what has personally worked for me, and what hasn't been effective. As I shared in the final tip, I even changed jobs twice during this time period and was able to implement the tips using a fresh lens. I acted as though I was only now picking up this book for the first time as a newbie networker and employed the tried-and-true email samples. I can attest, once again, that they work beautifully. My new colleagues were delighted when I reached out to get to know them, my former coworkers were pleased that I kept in touch, and so on and so forth.

As I also shared in the introduction, this book's writing overlapped with the global COVID-19 pandemic. For the first twenty-six years of my career, I worked from a physical office building every single day. The pandemic changed that, and I pivoted to working from home.

Admittedly, the first few weeks were challenging as I learned to adapt. Although I enjoyed saving time with no commute, and this frugal lady certainly appreciated saving money with no in-person coffee or lunch meetings, I wondered how I would continue to effectively network in my new environment. I'm happy to report that the tips indeed hold up splendidly in a work-from-home virtual setting.

You have the tools to just be yourself—really!—as you authentically network within your company. Even if you don't work at headquarters. Even if you work from home. And especially if, like me, you're an introvert.

Best wishes, and I'm rooting for your success!

ACKNOWLEDGMENTS

One of the delights of developing a strong network is that I have many people to thank.

I have had the most joyous and fulfilling career at AT&T, an extraordinary company made up of extraordinary people. You'll recall in my introduction I described that the origins of this book came from a presentation I had been giving for years which highlighted real emails that I had either sent to colleagues or they had sent to me. While they have each given me permission to share, for this book, I opted to change their names. Thank you to each of them for the inspiration that went into this book. Thank you to all of the amazing supervisors, peers, and mentors who have shaped my career and leadership style, many of whom I am fortunate to count as true friends in addition to colleagues.

I become emotional when I think about my family, who have supported me throughout my writing journey, and frankly, my whole life. I am overwhelmed with gratitude for the impact they have had on me.

To my dad, Steve, for being my original mentor and who always makes me feel like I'm doing everything right in life; to Jamie, who role-modeled what a successful female executive looked like.

To my mom, Marcy, who instilled in me my love of writing and grammar (and correcting other people's grammar) and for teaching me to listen, the foundational tenant of any relationship.

To my mother-in-law, Susan, for the sunshine and warmth she brought to my life; to my father-in-law, Jerry, for his humor and for teaching me to play my favorite game, backgammon.

To my incredible sisters, Rebecca and Alison, and their equally incredible husbands and children for years of laughter, memories, and support. To my sister-in-law, Jessica, and her family for the positivity and care. To my bonus sister, Kim, and her family for the love and encouragement.

My circle of friends has been nothing less than life-giving and sustaining. To Nicole C. for her deep insights and love of details; to Amy for her brilliant marketing and fashion advice; to Jen P. for her creativity; to Geri for her sound advice; to Bonnie for her excellent writing guidance; to Jen N. for always being up to try something new with me; to my CBI tribe, including Rabbi Charlie, Nicole F., Leslie, Caryn, and Stephanie for their never-ending friendship; and to Jordyn for being a constant source of light.

To my earliest readers, who provided invaluable coaching and gentle refinement along the way—Nicole C., Bill, Rebecca, and Andy. I could not have done this without them. To Steve A., who helped me crystalize my vision for the book. To Craig for his guidance and innovative ways to look at challenges.

Thank you to my team at Amplify Publishing including Lauren, Caitlin, and David, for helping to bring this book to life.

And finally, to my heart, pride, and joy—my children and husband—whose love and support I feel every single day. To Abigail for her wisdom, strength, and tenacity; to Ethan for his humor and easygoing nature; and to Jason, the love of my life, for helping me to approach opportunities in new ways, for guiding me to expand my limitations, and for evolving with me in all the best ways possible.

I love you all so much, and I'm filled with gratitude.

ABOUT THE AUTHOR

Rachel B. Simon is an executive at AT&T, one of the world's largest companies and most recognizable brands. She began her remarkable career as a college hire from the University of Texas and has served in key roles in privacy, finance, and customer care for almost three decades. As a popular speaker, she brings to life the importance of meaningful relationships and the power of internal networking for increased job and personal satisfaction. A consistent theme of her career has been mentoring, employee engagement, and diversity and inclusion and she has helped countless others expand their limiting beliefs around fulfillment, balance, and success in the workplace. She lives in Dallas with her husband, Jason, and is the proud mom to her two children, Abigail and Ethan.